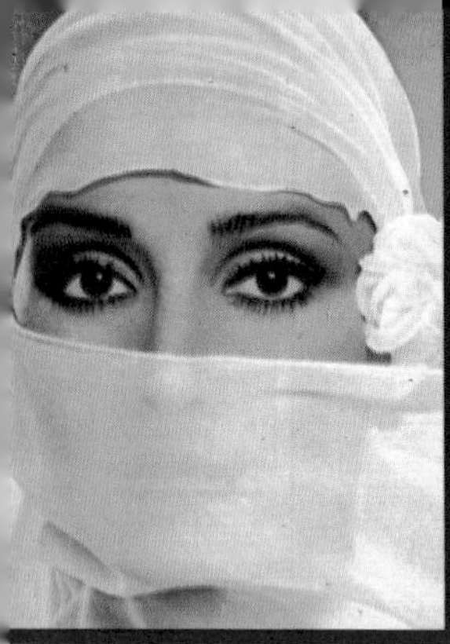

ARAB WORLD COOK BOOK

by Nahda Salah

By the name of God the Compassionate the merciful.

ARAB WORLD COOK BOOK

The book of One Thousand and One Delights.

Cooking and Text by Nahda S. Salah.
Photography by Basem S. Salah.

Published and distributed by Said Salah
International Publications Agencies
P.O. Box 70, Dhahran Airport
Dhahran, Saudi Arabia.

1st Publication Feb. 1973
2nd Publication Feb. 1975
3rd Publication Jun. 1977

Printed by
Tien Wah Press (Pte) Limit
977 Bukit Timah Road,
Singapore 21.

CONTENTS

To my mother, the master cook, who cooked all the dishes Photographed in this Book; and to my brother Basem, who Photographed them.

ALL YOU HAVE TO DO IS:

Follow the pictures and cook the articulated Arabian Delicacies which are the only rival to the Chinese and French cuisines; and are descended from mothers to daughters since the glamorous days of the Alhambra Palace of Granada-Andalusia.

Easy and simple recipes that make your neighbours and guests savour the aroma coming out from your kitchen.

When the conversation goes culinary this book will make you the star of your guests.

Vine leaves stuffed with rice, meat and spices.

See the recipe of this delicious dish at page No. 152.

THE NOBLE ART OF COOKING IN THE ARAB WORLD

Arab World cooking, though sometimes elaborate, is easy. Some of the dishes, such as stuffed vine leaves, may take sometime to prepare; but if you consider cooking to be a pleasurable and creative activity, you are adding to the enjoyment of serving and eating the dish, the peace and pleasure derived from rolling up the leaves. Women in the West like to knit while listening to music, or while sitting with their children. Could rolling with leaves and stuffing tomatoes not be yet another such soothing activity?

COOKING ARAB FOOD OUTSIDE THE ARAB LAND

The preparation of most of these dishes is short and simple. Some require lengthy cooking, but these often need very little work and hardly any attention as they can usually be cooked a day in advance and become richer in this way. Sometimes the cooking time can be greatly reduced by the use of modern labor-saving

Right: The Lebanese Kibbeh in tray and stuffed with meat, onion and pine seeds, page no. 53 and 59.

devices such as electric blenders or pressure cookers.

Arab food is economical, lamb and minced meat being the favorite meats. The recipes can give inspiration for subtle and exciting ways of cooking familiar and cheaper cuts of meat. The vegetables, used because of their abundance in the Middle East, are available almost everywhere today, either imported or home grown.

Spices can be found in most supermarkets as well as in Greek shops. Pine nuts and Hommus, not generally available in ordinary shops, can usually be found in all Greek shops, and in some delicatessens.

In the Middle East there is always a story behind the origin of each dish and listening to these stories is a fascinating experience. Culinary manuals in the Middle East have been found dating from the eighth and nineth centuries.

During those days a creative culinary genius flourished at the banquets of the notables, which became proverbial for their variety and lavishness. Manuals on the noble art of cooking are known to have been written at that time. Songs were sung about food, poems were written and legends born of the great feasts which featured in the Arabian Nights.

The Turks, Persian, Greek and other Middle Eastern nations sometimes claim most of our dishes, but from its Arabic name one can detect the authenticity of its Arabian origin.

SPICES:

Each country seems to have a favorite combination of spices or herbs. A favorite Meccan spice mixture is made up of one part hot pepper (cayenne), two parts of sweet pepper (paprika), and two parts of cinnamon. Another Arab favorite, called taklia, is ground coriander fried with crushed garlic, the smell of which trickles out through the door of every home during the blessed month of RAMADAN. Fresh coriander is a herb often used by Arabs in their salads and stews.

It is customary to place a bowl of fresh yoghurt on the table, to be eaten with such varied foods as ejje, stuffed vegetables, salads and kebabs. It is sometimes flavored with salt, mint, and crushed garlic.

GENERAL FEATURES OF THE FOOD OF THE ARAB WORLD

OIL:

All countries in the Arab World use olive oil for dishes which are to be eaten cold. For most deep frying, corn or nut oil is used, but for deep frying fish, olive oil is preferred. As a general practice, people like to fry or sauté their meat and vegetables before adding water to make stews and soups. These acquire a darker color and a somewhat richer flavor, while the meat,

sealed by the preliminary frying retains its juices.

It is suggested that after the initial trying out of a new recipe the reader should trust his taste and allow himself greater freedom in its preparation.

QUALITIES OF FOOD

In the past, some foods were believed to have high spirit qualities. Of foods which some old culinary veterans acknowledge to have a positive effect in stimulating amorous desires are: an asparagus omelet, fried onion omelet, camel's milk mixed with honey, eggs boiled with myrrh, coarse cinnamon and pepper, eggs chickpeas. Even today, a certain belief in the aphrodisiac powers of some foods still exists everywhere in the world.

Cooking in the Arab World is deeply traditional and an inherited art. Its virtues are loyalty and respect for custom and tradition, reflected in the unwavering attachment to the dishes of the past.

In Jordan, similar rules to these are added to Western manners in homes where Western habits of eating have been adopted, and certain actions and words reveal this attachment to ancient tradition. At buffet dinner parties in a Kuwaiti house, for example, the guests stood far away from the table and had to be urged and pressed to eat. Although the Western table manners are adopted, the old, Arab World manners and rules remain.

The Time to be

SOCIAL ASPECTS

The activities of cooking and eating reflect many subtly intricate facets of the Arabian character and way of life. They are intensely social activities, while the dishes hold within them centuries of local culture, art, and tradition.

Hospitality is a stringent duty all over the Arab World. Offer the guest food to eat even though you yourself are starving , is only one of a large number of sayings which serve to remind people of this duty.

The ultimate aim of civility and good manners is to please: to please one's guest or to please one's host. To this end one uses the rule strictly laid down by tradition: of welcome, generosity, affability, cheerfulness, and consideration for others.

When an Arab friend invites you, he entertains warmly and joyously. For him, to persuade a friend to stay for lunch is a triumph and precious honor. To entertain many together is to honor them all mutually. It is equally an honor to be a guest. Besides the customary obligations of cordiality and welcome, there is the need for the warmth of personal contact and

 Right: A Tunisian girl in her traditional dress.

cheerful company, the desire to congregate in groups, and the wish to please. It is common when preparing food to allow for an extra helping in case an unexpected guest should arrive.

If a guest comes unexpectedly, the host must never ask why he has come, but receive him with a smiling face and look of intense pleasure. After a ceremony of greetings, he should remark on the pleasure of seeing him and the honor of such a visit. The guest should never say rightaway why he has come, if there is a reason, but first inquire about the family, friends, and affairs of his host. The latter must treat his guests as though he were their servant; to quarrel with them would be a disgrace. He must never ask his guests if they would like food or drink, but provide these automatically, insisting that they have them and ignoring repeated refusals.

The first duty of a host is cheerfulness, a maxim strictly abided by. A host must amuse and entertain, provide light gossip, jokes, and occasionally, riddles and a little satire.

A guest, in turn, must also play his role correctly. He is expected to guard his voice, shorten his sight, and praise the food .

Left: The Kuwaiti traditional dress.
Right: The Jordanian traditional dress.

The Saudi Arabian traditional dress.

ʰe traditional dress of The United Arab Emerates.

It is customary for an emergency guest at first to refuse the food offered to him, but eventually give in on being urgently pressed. An invited guest must never refuse dishes which have already been sampled by others of the company, as this would put them in an uncomfortable position.

When a guest leaves, he must bless his host and he is under an obligation to speak well of him to others.

Cooks are constantly coaxed and encouraged to surpass themselves and to perfect family favorites. Cooking ability is rated highly among female accomplishments. One Arab saying goes: "A woman first holds her husband with a pretty face, then with cheerfulness, and by his tummy."

Weddings, religious festivals, new arrivals, in fact most occasions, call for a particular dish or delicacy, or even a whole range of specialties. If these are lacking when it is customary to include them, it is a cause for offense and gossip Criticism and disapproval are feared most by those who wish to impress and do the right or customary thing. This accounts for the fact that parties, though often extra ordinarily lavish and varied, are also repetitive within each community. No table could be without stuffed vine leaves, Tabbouleh, Kibbeh and Hommus, Mutabbal and the usual range of delicacies. How fearful one is of the critical gaze of guests searching for some specialty which is missing from the table.

ETIQUETTE OF FOOD IN THE ARAB WORLD

It is said that there is a language of flowers. In the Arab World there exists a language of food. A code of etiquette for serving and presenting particular dishes expresses subtle social distinctions. There are rules of procedure according to social and family status and age. A dignitary or the head of the family is served the best helping first. An alien guest is served before one who is a regular and familiar visitor to the house.

My brother Basem, the photographer of this book, and I fourteen years ago. Taken somewhere near the present site of the University of Petroleum and Minerals, Dhahran, Saudi Arabia from where Basem graduated last month.

In eating, a strict code of etiquette is observed. In the teachings of Islam it is necessary to say: "In the name of God" when beginning to eat and to say: "To God be thanks" when finished. It is also necessary to wash the hands before eating; to sit at the left of the table; to take small pieces; to chew the food well and silently; and not to gaze at the others at the table with you. These rules form the traditional basis for the table manners of the majority of the people of the Arab. When the meal is finished, guests leave the table to go through the handwashing ceremony again and to partake of coffee or tea.

The religion of Islam is the most important part of the Arab World culture and the main foundation of the customs and traditions of the region. The code of religion is derived mainly from the Quran, which serves the faithful as a model and rule of life in every particular way.

In actual fact, the following are forbidden:

1. Animals dead before they are slaughtered
2. Blood
3. Pig's flesh
4. Alcohol or liquors

An animal that is killed for the food of man must be slaughtered in a particular manner, otherwise it is listed with the forbidden. The person who is about to do it must say: "In the name of God, God is most great", and then cut its throat.

RAMADAN, THE MONTH OF SELF DISCIPLINE, MEDITATION AND PRAYERS AT DAYTIME, AND DELICACIES AND FESTIVALS AT NIGHT.

During the 30 days of the month of RAMADAN, Moslems fast from dawn to dusk. It is the time when daily routine reverses itself and conventional day-time activities become nocturnal. Housewives serve their families their first meal of the day shortly after maghreb (sunset), signalled by a cannon shot which signifies the end of the day's fasting at fifteen minutes to seven in the evening.

In Saudi Arabia and the Gulf States, the first meal will nearly always include two traditional dishes, Sambousick (page 203) or three date fruits, and Shourba (soup). In the rest of the Arab countries, fasters start with Kamareddine (the fruit of apricot, smashed and dried, and then melted with water and ice to become a healthy refreshment).

An Arab housewife knows that the meal must be both nourishing and filling, particularly if Ramadan falls during a hot summer. Lasting 29 to 30 days, the length of time and season of the year is determined by the lunar calendar. Family tradition prescribes how the fast is broken. Some families eat their first main meal immediately following the cannon signal. Others gather in large family groupings and share liquid refreshments (Kamareddine) followed later by the main meal.

But most follow the way of the Prophet Mohammad who broke his fast with dates, prayed for an hour and then partook of a meal. Dates are always included in Ramadan meals for both their historical significance and their high sugar content.

Ramadan is looked upon as a time to develop self discipline. Moslems always feel more alert in both mind and body during Ramadan. Children begin observing the fast at the age of twelve or puberty. It also is a time for goodies at meal-times.

In Saudi Arabia, Kuwait, Qatar, Bahrain and the United Arab Emirates, Kamareddine apricot nectar) is made and drunk from glasses heavily scented with ouda (sandalwood), burning in a Moubkhara (incense burner) which is brought to the dining area when the meal is finished.

In addition to usual seasoning, soft yellow balls of Mistakah, Arabic gum, are added to pots of lamb meat. Besides adding taste, Mistakah acts as a thickening agent and also produces a delicious scent if burned in place of ouda.

No Ramadan meal is complete without the special sweets Gatayef (page 323), a round pastry with walnuts and raisins, and Kunafah, a shoelace pastry stuffed with sweet white cheese and syrup.

Some families depart from tradition and occasionally serve Margouk, a genuine Saudi dish from the Nejd containing huge whole wheat pancakes.

Travellers and the sick are excluded from fasting during Ramadan but it is expected missed days will be made-up for prior to the next Ramadan period.

Following the first meal, parties, large family gatherings and visiting usually take place until about 3 a.m. Then a second large meal is served in preparation of Fajr, the cannon shot signalling the start of a new day of fasting.

Right: A village bakery in Bahrain.

AN ALPHABET OF ARABIAN FOOD

A compendium of remembered tastes and pleasures and a few facts:

AUBERGINE — Perhaps the most oriental of vegetables, but a staple whose size and shape dictate the dish — Cardinal Manning used to have five courses of fish during Lent; one could have 14 courses of aubergine without mortifying the flesh — in a puree with sesame paste, in fritters, in stews, stuffed in several ways, fried, with garlic and yoghurt as a salad, pickled — aubergines having very little taste themselves, are a perfect vehicle for all the spices and flavours of the orient.

APRICOTS — called *mish mish* — blooming and scented at the end of a meal — cooked in a fruit soup — dried into sheets of paste that look like a shellac that would forever remain tacky — cooked with chicken and lamb in Persian dishes.

ALMONDS — blanched, roasted, salted and eaten with drinks — pureed as a sauce for fish — a decoration in a variety of sweet milk puddings — in the spring, beautifully arranged on barrows in their green skins.

ALLSPICE — or Jamaican pepper — a pepper

that seems a combination of cloves, nutmeg and cinnamon — gives meat and vegetable dishes a characteristic Middle Eastern flavour.
BREAD — the round, flat and hollow loaves are used as fork and spoon and napkin — mountain bread is like thin sheets of coarse brown paper — bread in sesame sprinkled crescent shapes is sold on the streets with a mixture of salt and herbs to eat with it.
BURGHUL — cracked wheat — always soaked in water — used in salads like tabbouli — mixed with lamb in kibbeh — cooked in broth with a scrap of garlic, a delicious vegetable on its own.

BRAINS — lightly boiled, sliced in a salad of oil and lemon garnished with black olives and tomatoes — said to be good for the brains.
CHICKEN, CIRCASSIAN — boiled, with a thick sauce of pounded walnuts, decorated with oil coloured red with paprika.
CORIANDER — green leaves, a spicier sort of parsley used in salads and stews — the seeds are crushed and fried with garlic as a flavouring for Egyptian dishes.

CARDAMON — the pod sometimes floats in the small cups of thick Turkish coffee — the seed, pulverized, flavours yoghurt in a delicious dish of offal.

CUCUMBER — cut in thin sticks and salted as an hors d'oeuvre — sliced in a cold soup of yoghurt with crushed garlic and dried mint.

Right: Bedouins coffee pots on a br
box ornamented with brass.

CARROT JUICE — squeezed on the spot and drunk as a restorative in the middle of a Beirut *souk.*

COFFEE — very thick and sweet, or *masbout,* medium — bedouin coffee boiled until it is a bitter coffee essence and drunk in infinitesimal amounts in cups, without handles, decorated with golden Turkish crescents, made in China.

DOLMAS — stuffed vegetables: aubergines, courgettes, tomatoes, green peppers, onions, vine leaves, all filled with a mixture of rice and mutton nuts and raisins, onions and tomatoes, herbs and spices.

DATES — from Mecca, eaten on a summer evening, heavy with the scent of jasmine, in a garden in Beirut — stuffed with almonds and sugared for a feast.

EGYPTIAN CAVIAR — batarekh, dried, salted grey mullet roe in thin slices with oil and lemon — a strange taste that one might possibly acquire — served at the coronation feast of James II in 1685.

EGGS — said to have aphrodisiac qualities — fried until the edges are crisp and eaten out of the pan they taste like no others — they are dyed red for the New Year, yellow with saffron to garnish a

dish of Persian rice, or cooked long and slowly with coffee to be eaten with a dish of Egyptian brown beans.

FOUL — the Egyptian national dish — brown beans and a handful of red lentils cooked very slowly, perhaps overnight on a primus stove, dressed with lemon or lime juice and oil, cumin, salt and pepper — eaten in the midmorning with spring onions, or anytime.

FIGS — Freya Stark carried fig sandwiches on a cross-country exploration of the Druse territory — fig jam with cream cheese.

FRUIT SYRUPS — mint, mulberry, orange, rose, tamarind and strawberry — diluted with iced water and offered to guests in the summer.
GARLIC — thought to have healing properties and to ward off the evil eye — gives much innocent pleasure pounded with oil and lemon as a sauce for grilled chicken.
HERBS — eating fresh green herbs ensures happiness and prosperity.
HOMMOUS — a Lebanese speciality — a puree of chick-peas with lemon, garlic and sesame paste — more luxuriously served hot with oil and fried pine nuts poured over it.
HOSPITALITY — perhaps the finest Arab tradition — guests are always made to feel welcomed — always offered something to eat and drink — if there is not more than enough, there is not enough.
HALWA —a sweet made of sesame paste.
HONEY — the adhesive ingredient of many Arabic pastries.
ICES — eaten in the garden of Groppi's cafe in Cairo where gentlemen in slightly shabby white linen suits read their newspapers — they are made of every imaginable fruit, tangerine and mango and a beautiful pale green one with

Left: The healthy breakfast dish "Foul", very popular all over the Arab world.

pistachios — a dark mulberry ice eaten out of a little paper cone in a *souk* in Alepp.

JEBNE — a white cheese eaten with black olives for breakfast — or when a few days old, sliced and fried as a *mezze* dish. A Palestinian specialty.

JERUSALEM SALAD — finely chopped salad of tomato, cucumber, spring onions, radish, and perhaps hot green pepper, with a dressing of oil, lemon, and sesame paste.

KIBBEH — a paste of lamb pounded in a mortar and mixed with cracked wheat and onions — eaten raw with mint and spring onions — cooked in a variety of loaves and meatballs.

KEBABS — chunks of lamb on a skewer, marinated or not, with or without onions and tomatoes, but cooked over charcoal.

KADIFI — a festive pastry that looks like shredded wheat stuffed with pistachios nuts and moistened with honey.

LEMONS — used more often than vinegar as a salad dressing.

LENTILS — a salad with oil and lemon — a soup with rice and fried onions on top — a stew with spinach.

LAHMA BI AJEEN — a sort of Arabic pizza with minced lamb, onions and the ubiquitous allspice.
MASBAHIT EL DARWISH — monk's rosary — this man was so poor that he only had one onion, one tomato, one aubergine. The dish is a stew using a bit of every vegetable available and some chunks of lamb — all sautéed first, then baked in the oven — the vegetables and meat can also be threaded on a skewer and broiled.
MINT — always used as a decoration and garnish — with lamb — in salads.
MUNKACZINA — salad of orange slices and onion rings and black olives, salt, pepper and oil — Anatole France liked it.

MELOKHIA — another Egyptian national dish, old as the Pharoahs — a green spinach-like vegetable that becomes glutinous when cooked — must be chopped minutely with two handled chopper (dried *melokhia* may be used). A chicken is boiled in rich stock, the chicken is removed, the stock is strained and the melokhia cooked quickly in it — it should then be evenly suspended throughout the broth — a piquant garlic sauce is added — garlic crushed in salt is fried with coriander and cayenne — the soup is served first, then the chicken with rice cooked in some of the stock.

SHEESHAH — a utensil for smoking tobacco through a water filter — has become the symbol of oriental dolce far niente — brought on after the meal in old-fashioned houses and restaurants.

NUTS — in huge glass jars they entice the customer into the shop — walnuts, pine nuts, pistachios, almonds, hazel nuts, peanuts and melon seeds — for cooking or just for eating — sometimes sold in caramelised clusters as a sweet.

OLIVES — shades of green and brown — stuffed or crushed and spiced with garlic or coriander — Lawrence Durrell says they taste of the whole Mediterranean — proper housewives used to pride themselves on making their own olive oil.

ORANGES — sold and served with the stem and a leaf or two — infinitely more appetising than without.

POMEGRANATE — the juice pounded with walnuts makes an ambrosial sauce in which to cook a Persian dish of wild ducks called *fezanjan.*

PILAF — rice cooked with other ingredients: saffron or tumeric — any combination of mutton, onions, chick-peas, pine nuts, currants, chicken, almonds, apricots.

PICKLES — green peppers and cucumber — turnips red with beet juice — aubergines with garlic — also in enormous jars to lure one salivating off the street and into the restaurant.

QUINCE — a jam or in paste squares stuck with almonds and served with coffee.

ROSEWATER — a few drops to perfume the coffee — also accounts for the perfume of Turkish Delight, thought by some to be the quintessential east.

ROSEPETAL JAM — tops the cream that tops the *ataif,* the Arab pancake that is a traditional wedding dish.

RED MULLET — fried whole and eaten with lemon wedges at a rough table under a bamboo shade in a restaurant by the sea where the service is negligible and the marine blue view is all.

SHAWARMA — thin slices of lamb on a turning vertical spit with an onion and a lemon at the top — pieces are cut from the outside and the spit keeps turning so that everyone gets crispy bits in his packet of Arab bread — a tomato, mint and onion mixture is optional.

SESAME — from which is made the paste

tahini — essential ingredient in purees of chick-peas, aubergine, chard — a salad dressing or a sauce for fish or with lemon juice and spices as a salad on its own.
SAMNA — oriental or clarified butter — supposed to give the food its special taste — nowadays considered rather heavy, so ordinary butter or oil is substituted for cooking.
TARATOUR — a thick mayonnaise made from pureed pine nuts or walnuts, breadcrumbs, garlic and lemon — thinned with fish stock this makes a gala dish out of any white fish.
TABBOULI — I once stayed in a small Lebanese mountain village whose population consisted almost entirely of old women, waiting for letters from Australia and Africa and America. They spent whole mornings making a communal *tabbouli,* washing and chopping the parsley, tomatoes, spring onions and mint. They told stories while they worked. The salad is mixed with soaked *bourghol,* seasoned with lemon and oil and eaten with Romaine lettuce leaves. It seemed not a bad way to grow old.

UTENSILS — one still sees beautiful cooking utensils — variously patterned cake molds of apricot wood — beaten copper vessels big enough to cook an enemy in — a colander with the holes in parsley shapes, huge flat trays for sweets — copper pots shaped like birds for Bedouin coffee — beautifully curved wire egg baskets.

WATERMELON — the most beautiful fruit — neatly piled hills of them — some sliced open for allure — keeping cool under a canopy of hessian sacks — a tasty combination with toasted bread and cheese.

YOGHURT — delicious in its brown earthenware pots — a cooling agent for almost any highly spiced oriental dish — Persians add soda water and drink it.

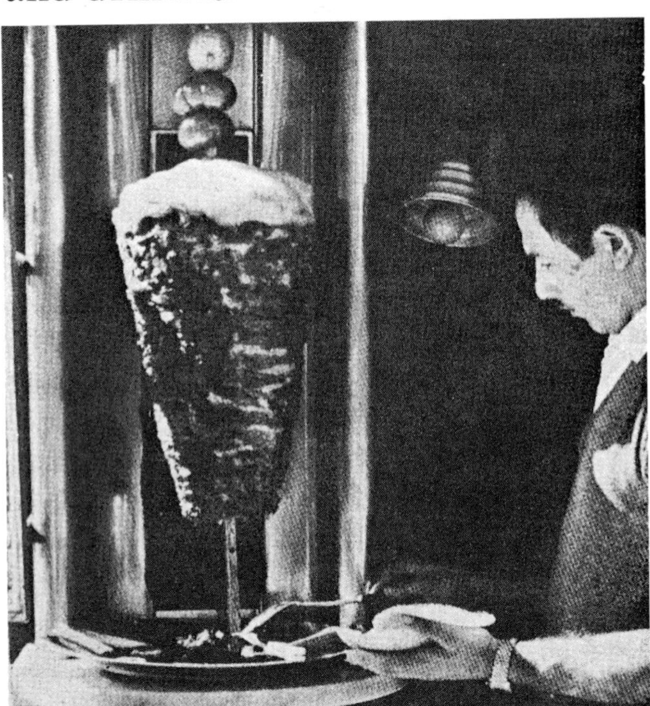

The famous Shawerma, the creation of Arab world of cooks.

THE TRADITIONAL SAUDI DELICACIES OF "SALEEK", "NEEFAH", "NADI", "KOUZI" AND "RUZ BOKHARI"

The most famous and interesting Saudi delicacies are served in public kitchens which specialise in preparing and cooking the traditional Saudi dishes of lamb and rice.

There are about half-a-dozen most popular variations of the classic lamb and rice dish in the Arabian cuisine, each with its own name, ingredients, method of cooking and presentation. Some of the dishes have a recognised regional heritage-"NEEFAH" for instance is a traditional speciality of Taif, "NADI" is said to come from the Nejd, and among the Bedouin cooking lamb on a spit-"SHAWERMA" is a most favoured method these days. However the Saudi dishes have now spread far and wide in Jeddah, Mecca, Medina and in Taif's public kitchens the customers can usually state his preference. Tradition has it that the customer provides his own lamb which is delivered live to the kitchen where it is slaughtered and prepared for cooking. The owner of the kitchen provides the rest of the ingredients — rice, spices, butter and so forth —

for an all inclusive cost of around Saudi Riyals 50.

The method of cooking known as "NEEFAH" is accepted by many as the best way of cooking lamb certainly the results are said to be exceptionally tender. It can be done both above the ground in a large clay oven or, in a hole in the ground, which is lined with clay bricks. Burning wood is placed in the bottom of the hole or clay oven and a large bowl of rice is lowered on top of it. A whole lamb on a spit is then placed in the oven vertically and a heavy lid, or sometimes earth, is placed on top to seal in the steam. As the lamb slowly cooks in the hot oven it releases fat and juices which fall into the pot of rice below. As it is the heat given off by the smouldering wood which cooks the lamb and rice, the sealed lid cannot be taken off until the lamb is completely cooked — a matter of judgement on the part of the cooks in charge.

"NADI" and "KOUZI" are two more variations on the theme and in both methods the lamb is cooked in a large pot over a fire (electric burners are now used in some kitchens) and the rice is later cooked in the gravy and juices from the cooked lamb. The major difference between the two dishes is that "KOUZI" is one dish — the lamb and rice are served together on one enormous platter, and "NADI" is two separate dishes, one of rice and the other of lamb. Different accompanying vegetable dishes are also served, distinguishing one dish from the other.

When lamb is served with rice cooked in milk it is called "SALIK" which is favoured when there are special occasions to be celebrated.

THE ARAB OMELET, CALLED EJJE

It is more like a cake. Thick and rich, with an infinite variety of vegetables.

MELOKHIA

Melokhia is another Arab World national dish. Since fresh Melokhia leaves are hard to find outside the Middle East, it is suggested that you use the dried Melokhia, readily available in most Greek shops.

FALAFEL

Falafel is an Arabic name which means hot spicy cookies. It is one of the specialties of all the Arab World. Falafel is a meal of which rich and poor alike never tire. It is welcomed at all times, for lunch, after lunch, or supper. It is the Hot Dogs of the Middle East. In Egypt, it is called TA'AMIA.

KIBBEH

Kibbeh is a mixture of fine cracked wheat or burghul, grated onion, and ground lamb pounded to a paste. Eaten raw, it is called Kibbeh naye. The same paste can be fried or grilled. In Kibbeh bil Soniah, a layer of minced meat filling is sandwiched between two layers of Kibbeh and baked in the oven. Stuffed Kibbeh are hollow, oval or long egg-shaped shells of the same paste, filled with minced meat mixture and deep-fried. This last type has innumerable variations: the outer Kibbeh shell is sometimes made with seasoned cracked wheat alone.

You can use a very fine grinder to save some of the pounding (or an electric blender as suggested for meatball mixtures), and a machine has recently been developed in Lebanon which takes care of the whole operation.

Kibbeh is the great traditional and national dish in Syria and Lebanon. The daily life of the kitchen cooks revolves around its preparation, a dramatic ritual.

Kibbeh Mahshe torpedo shaped

bbeh in tray.

In the Middle East, soups are often eaten as a meal in themselves, accompanied by Arab bread. Rich with vegetables, meat, legumes, and rice, they are sometimes indistinguishable from stews, except for the fact that they have very much more liquid.

Calf's feet or sheep's feet are added for their gelatinous quality. Legumes — lentils, chick-peas, yellow split peas, dried green peas, and haricot and fava beans — lend themselves beautifully to make thick, creamy soups, delicately enhanced by spices, garlic, and fresh herbs. There are infinite combination of spinach and lentils, spinach and meat balls, yoghurt and barley, yoghurt and spinach, and so on. Chicken stocks are sometimes thickened with beaten egg yolks and lemon, and fish stocks with egg yolks and vinegar, while meat stocks are made richer with a marrow bone.

The therapeutic qualities of yoghurt are legendary, for it fights and destroys the harmful germs that breed in the intestines and cause many diseases. As a blood purifier it is excellent, it gives a clear skin and sparkling eyes. It induces sleep and calms the nerves and has a remarkable effect on historical subjects. Medical observations have proved that the yoghurt bacillus remains alive even after the passage through the intestines whilst the bacillus of other milk products cannot survive this test. Middle East peasants, some of them claiming to be over one hundred years old, attribute their longevity to eating yoghurt daily.

The Middle East is noted for its oil wells, but it is primarily an agricultural area. Where there is wealth the quality of the people's food increases, and the great banquets of the early Arabs produced many of the dishes still famous today. The whole roasted lamb, or the young suckling calf, stuffed with rice and exotic herbs, while never losing their appeal, gave way to more specialised dishes.

Meat and vegetables are sometimes served together, but generally speaking each is a course in itself. Many vegetable dishes are cooked in olive oil and served cold with a squeeze of lemon. Meat is thought best served by itself, without accompaniment save, perhaps, salad. Rice, the king of dishes to a Middle Eastern is always served alone. Sweets and desserts tend to be heavy, a factor again determined by climate, since many Middle East countries have hard winters.

BORGHUL is made by boiling the grains and drying them. The process brings out the cereal flavour of the wheat. Burghul goes well with minced lamb, either raw or cooked, and is used as a substitute for rice.

THE RICE flavour of the Arab World is absolutely the best you have ever tasted. In its plain boiled form, it reaches the table a perfection of texture seldom found anywhere else.

THE LEBANESE MAZA: For those who are careless about weight control, one of the more fascinating spreads, pleasing both to the eye and the appetite is the Lebanese Maza. A maza is composed of a number of small dishes (anywhere from four to forty) containing hors d'oeuvres that are nibbled on along with the popular Yansoon flavored grape essence called arek. A maza will include nuts, tart fruits, salted seeds, any number of cheeses, salads, marinated bone marrow, cooked and raw liver, cucumbers, tomatoes, other greens, a whole gamut of vegetables cooked in olive oil (food cooked in olive oil are more delicious left cold and one day old, so leftovers are perfect for the purpose), tabbouleh and kubbeh (specialties with a cracked wheat base), pickles, olives, seafood, preserves and so on according to a hostess's ingenuity and flair. It is a wonderful social institution that at its best goes on for hours.

TURKISH COFFEE

In Lebanon, Syria and Jordan, Turkish coffee is served, always in small cups. It is brewed in varying styles and with different degrees of sweetness. A good hostess still takes real pride in the quality of the coffee that is offered in her home. In public places or business offices you can order it to your taste. It can be **MURRAH** (bitter) **SUKKAR ALIL** (little sugar), or **MAZBOUT** (just right).
But whatever your preference and no matter where you are, in office or home, among the rich or humble, in a remote village or the bustle of a town office, you can always count on a cup of coffee, the one unfailing sign that the guest is still esteemed and honored in the Arab World.

North African, Turkish and Iranian recipes are not mentioned in this book, but their cooking does in fact resemble the Arab World food because of the historic influence of Islamic culture in their areas.

When compared with the dishes of the other countries, Arab dishes, despite the richer taste are easier to cook and can be the attraction of your dinner table.

If this book could become a good companion in your kitchen, your food will become the talk of the family.

MAHSHI means **STUFFED.** In Turkish it is **DOLMA.** The variations of **MAHSHI** are: Huge onion hollowed out and stuffed with meat and rice.

Courgettes, eggplants or tomatoes hollowed out and filled with delicious stuffing.

Steamed vine leaves stuffed, each with about 1 tablespoon of rice, meat and tomato mixture.

Potatoes stuffed with meat, onion and pine kernels.

Roast chicken stuffed with rice, onions, pine kernels, currants etc. and steam-cooked on low heat.

Solid Measure

English

1 lb. Butter or other fat
1 lb. Flour
1 lb. Granulated or Castor Sugar
1 lb. Icing or Confectioners' Sugar
1 lb. Brown (moist) Sugar
1 lb. Golden Syrup or Treacle
1 lb. Rice
1 lb. Dried Fruit
1 lb. Chopped Meat (finely packed)
1 lb. Lentils or Split Peas
1 lb. Coffee (unground)
1 lb. Soft breadcrumbs
1/2 oz. Flour
1 oz. Flour
1 oz. Sugar
1/2 oz. Butter
1 oz. Golden Syrup or Treacle
1 oz. Jam or Jelly

American

2 cups
4 cups
2 cups
3 cups
2 1/2 cups
1 cup
2 cups
2 cups
2 cups
2 cups
2 1/2 cups
4 cups
1 level tablespoon*
1 heaped tablespoon
1 level tablespoon
1 level tablespoon smoothed off
1 level tablespoon
1 level tablespoon
* must be proper measuring tablespoon

French Weights and Measures

It is difficult to convert to French measures with absolute accuracy, but 1 oz. is equal to approximately 30 grammes, 2 lb. 3 oz. to 1 kilogramme. For liquid measure, approximately 1 3/4 English pints may be regarded as equal to 1 litre: 1 demi-litre is half a litre, and 1 decilitre is one-tenth of a litre.

Sorting the qualities of hommos by an Arab housewife.

Follow the sequence of pictures to cook the Saudi Arabian delicacy "Roz Bil — Laham".

Start by cutting two onions as follows:

Fry the onion, t
add butter.

Add three cups
of the water
with which you
boiled the meat

Add salt.

Put the rice.

Then add the already boiled meat.

Add two tins of tomato sauce or equivalence.

Mix everything.

Cook until the rice is good, use your taste.

Add the fried nuts on top of rice.

Follow the pictures and you will have articulated the famous Saudi Arabian Samboosa (see page for the recipe).

pare the dough
m your prefered
ur brand.

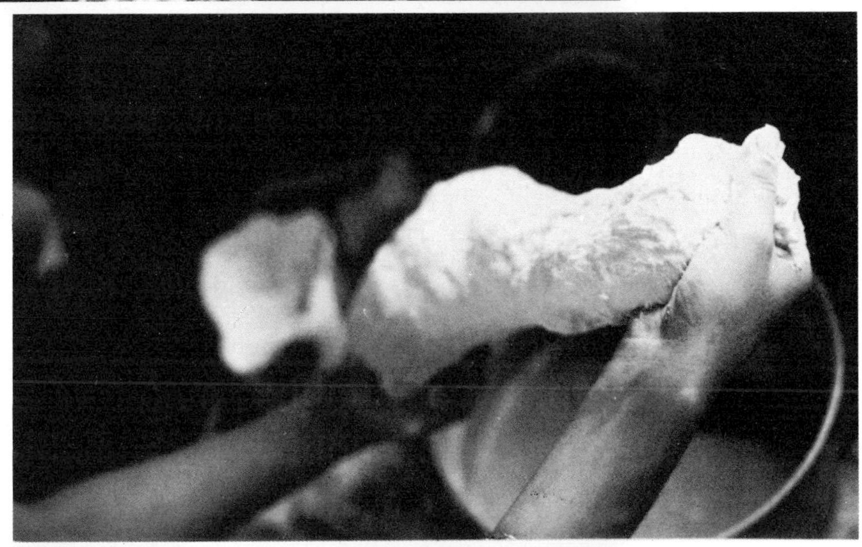

Cover the dough with a piece of cloth for an hour.

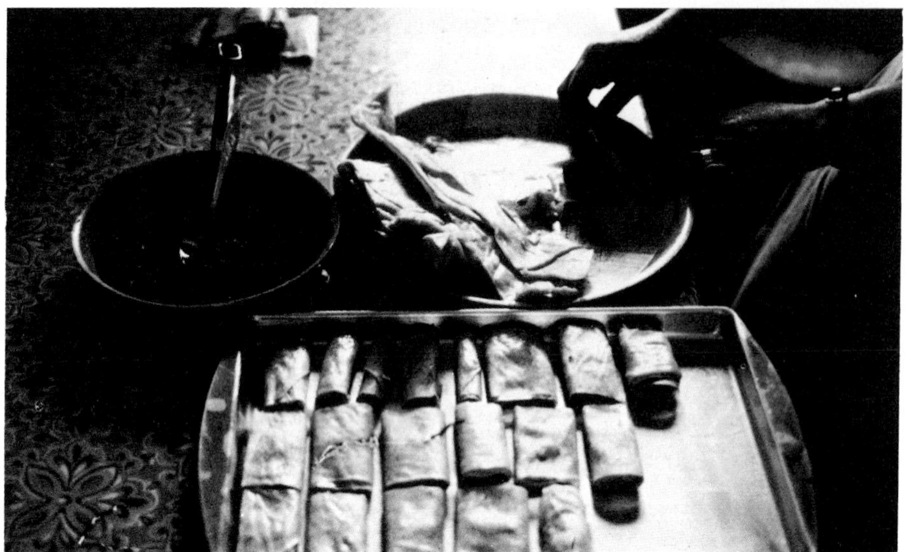

Stuff the do with meat a pine seeds, put it into t oven.

Another delicacy popular all over the Arab world, Lahm — Biajeen (see recipe page 207).

The way to boil cabbages to become tender. Later the leaves are stuffed with rice and meat and cooked (see recipe on page 157)

GENERAL
ELECTRIC

THICK VEGETABLE SOUP

Saudi Arabia

In Arabia the dishes are selected to complement each other in taste as, for example, vegetable soup, a curry of chicken, fried fish, sliced raw carrot with hot pepper sauce.

1/2 cup diced meat or chicken
1 1/2 cups meat or chicken stock
1 bay leaf
salt to taste
4 cups shredded vegetables (cabbage, green beans, cauliflower, carrots, lima beans)
1 tablespoon chopped green pepper
1 tablespoon chopped onion
1 1/2 cups milk

COMBINE meat, stock, bay leaf, and salt in kettle. Bring to boil.

ADD vegetables. Cover

SIMMER (20 to 30 minutes) until vegetables are tender.

ADD milk gradually. Cook, stirring for 2 minutes

YIELD 6 servings

BEAN SOUP

Lebanon

This is best made with large brown beans.

TO SERVE 6 — 8

12 oz. brown beans
2 lb. shin of beef, complete with bone and marrow
2 — 3 pints (U.S. 5 — 7 1/2 cups) water
3 leeks
2 oz. butter
salt to taste

Soak the beans overnight. Cut up the shin of beef and cook it (with carrots, onion, herbs and bay leaf, if you like) to make a good broth, skimming off the fat from time to time. (This takes about 2 hours). Cook the beans in boiling salted water for 30 minutes. Cut up the leeks and sauté them in butter. Drain the water from the beans and the butter from the leeks and add beans and leeks to the broth. Add more water, if necessary. Cook until the beans are tender — about 1 hour. Put the soup through a strainer — to remove bones, etc. — and then through a sieve, rubbing the beans through and as much of the meat as possible — they should provide the soup's thickening. Taste and season. When required, reheat the soup.

LENTIL SOUP

Shawrabat Adas — *Syria and Lebanon*

2 cups dried lentils
3 quarts water
2 medium onions, sliced
2 teaspoons salt
1 pound raw spinach, chopped
2 tablespoons lemon juice

SOAK lentils in water and cover in deep kettle overnight. Drain.
ADD water, onions, and salt
SIMMER for 2 hours, or until tender
ADD spinach. Cook for 10 minutes longer
ADD lemon juice before serving
YIELD 8 servings

SHORBAT YAKHNI

(Asparagus with Sour Cream)

Common to most Middle East countries

TO SERVE 4

2 lb. asparagus
4 teaspoons parsley, finely chopped
2 teaspoons chives
4 hard-boiled eggs
1/2 pint sour cream
1 teaspoon paprika

Clean asparagus by breaking off hard ends of stalks and removing any tough scales. Wash and tie in bundles of 12's. Stand upright in boiling salted water, cover and cook for 5 minutes. Strain and refill pan with fresh boiling water. Cover and cook over moderate heat for 30 minutes. Strain once more.

Arrange on a hot serving dish, chop roughly and pile on top and sprinkle with chives. Whisk the cream and pour over. Decorate with the parsley and a sprinkling of paprika. Serve immediately.

CREAM OF ONION SOUP

Kuwait

TO SERVE 6

3 lb. onions, sliced
2 pints white stock
1 bay leaf
1 gill single cream
salt to taste
3 tablespoons corn oil
2 cloves
1 leaf sage
2 oz. flour
1 teaspoon freshly ground white pepper

Heat oil and fry onions for 15 minutes over low heat. Let them soften but do not allow to brown. Bring stock to boil and add to onions, with cloves, seasoning and herbs. Simmer for 1 1/2 hours. Press through a fine sieve, return puree to saucepan and stir in the flour, first mixed to a paste with a little water. Cook until thickens, stirring frequently. Just before serving, add the cream.

VEGETABLE SOUP

Syria, Lebanon, Palestine

TO SERVE 6

1 lb. beef
1 large onion, chopped
2 stalks white celery
1 large potato, sliced
1 red pepper, seeded and sliced
1 teaspoon chopped dill
2 pints water
salt and pepper
2 tablespoons olive oil
2 young carrots, sliced
4 oz. white cabbage
1 tablespoon tomato puree
2 tablespoons chopped parsley
1/2 pint tarragon vinegar
2 pints bouillon

Heat oil in large saucepan and fry onion until lightly browned. Cut meat into small cubes and fry with onions for a further 10 minutes. Shake pan frequently to prevent onions sticking.

Add vegetables and cook another 5 minutes. Add water and stock, celery, tomato puree and seasoning, cover tightly and simmer over low heat for 2 1/2 hours. During last few minutes add the vinegar. Add, last of all, the dill and parsley. Serve immediately.

SHORBAT EL-JABAL (Groves of Paradise Soup)

Syria

TO SERVE 6

1 lb. white fish
2 onions, chopped
3 egg yolks
1 teaspoon tarragon
salt to taste
1 tablespoon rock salt
1 oz. plain flour
3 tablespoons olive oil
1 lemon juice
ground white pepper
few springs parsley

Put water in a saucepan, add rock salt and bring to boil. Put in cleaned fish and simmer for 10 minutes. Strain and keep the stock. Skin fish and flake off flesh from bones. Cut into small pieces and leave aside.

Reheat stock in which fish was cooked, mix flour with little water to form thin paste and add to stock. Boil for 5 minutes, stirring frequently, then remove from heat.

Fry onions in olive oil until transparent but not brown. Add pieces of fish, herbs and seasoning and cook for a further 7 minutes. Shake pan to prevent burning. Add this to the fish liquor and bring to boiling point.

Beat egg yolks for 2 minutes, add lemon juice and beat 1 minute more. Add a few tablespoons of the hot stock, stir well then pour the whole into the saucepan. Heat thoroughly but do not allow to boil. Serve hot, garnished with chopped parsley.

PUMPKIN SOUP

Syria, Lebanon and Jordan

TO SERVE 6 — 8

2 lb. shin of beef
vegetables for stock (see recipe)
2 — 2 1/2 pints (U.S. 5 — 6 1/4 cups) water
pumpkin (about 1 lb.)
2 oz. flour
2 oz. butter
salt to taste

Cook the beef, cut up, as in the recipe for bean soup. Skin the pumpkin and cut it up. Cook it with the beef. Strain the broth and then put it through a sieve. Make a white *roux* with the flour and the butter. Gradually whisk in the pumpkin broth. Season. If you like, you can keep a little of the pumpkin, cut it in dice and poach it in boiling water, so that the pieces are cooked but still firm, and add them as a garnish to the soup.

DOUGHNUTS WITH LABAN

Syria, Lebanon and Jordan

TO SERVE 4

2 1/5 lbs. best quality flour
2 pts. laban (yoghurt which is a little sour)
1 tbs. soda
1 2/5 oil for frying (Mazola, Wesson, etc.)
3 1/3 lbs. sugar (for syrup)
2 oz. rose water
1 oz. lemon juice (for syrup)
2 1/5 pts. boiling water (for syrup)

Sift flour with soda and a pinch of salt. Add laban gradually and knead well. Put oil in skillet — put over high heat.

Take a little of the dough into the hand, and, with a spoon cut dough in shape of large marbles. Drop these in hot oil. Turn the ball-shaped doughnuts till they are golden all round. Drop them into the syrup which has been prepared before-hand. Stir doughnuts in the syrup, then take them out onto a platter or tray. Repeat this operation till all the dough has been fried. Serve hot with syrup or without.

SALKHA (A Herb Sauce with Olive Oil)

Lebanon

6 tablespoons olive oil
1 teaspoon finely chopped shallot
1/2 teaspoon tarragon, finely chopped
1/2 teaspoon chives, finely chopped
1/2 teaspoon dry mustard
1/2 teaspoon salt
3 tablespoons tarragon vinegar
1 teaspoon parsley, finely chopped
1/2 teaspoon chervil, finely chopped
1 teaspoon gherkin, finely chopped
1/2 teaspoon icing sugar
1/2 teaspoon cayenne pepper

Mix the oil and seasoning and add the vinegar drop by drop, stirring all the time. Add all the other ingredients, a little at a time, still stirring between each addition. Leave aside for 12 hours then strain through butter muslin, when the sauce is ready for use.

TOSSED SALAD

Salatat Khodar — *Syria*

1/2 head lettuce, torn into pieces
1 cucumber sliced, tomatoes cut in wedges
1 tablespoon dried mint
4 springs parsley, chopped
3 tablespoons olive oil
2 tablespoons lemon juice
1/2 teaspoon salt

COMBINE lettuce, cucumber, tomatoes, mint, and parsley. Toss
BEAT together olive oil and lemon juice
ADD with salt to salad. Toss
YIELD 3 to 4 servings

EGGPLANT SALAD

Jordan

1 eggplant
1/4 cup mayonnaise
1 small onion, chopped
salt
black pepper
lemon juice

BAKE eggplant at 350°F for 1 hour. Cool
PEEL and cube
FORCE through sieve or use electric blender.
ADD remaining ingredients, season to taste. Mix well.
YIELD 4 servings
VARIATION: Combine with diced cucumber and tomato.

HANIM SALATA (My Lady's Salad)

Damascus

TO SERVE 6

1 lb. cooked chicken
3 hard-boiled eggs, quartered
1 tablespoon wine vinegar
6 spring onions, chopped
3 stalks white celery
12 black olives
heart of white cabbage
salt and pepper
1/2 pint wine dressing

Shred cabbage and celery very finely, mix with the onions and seasoning, stir in the vinegar and arrange at the bottom of a salad bowl. Cover with the shredded chicken and the hard-boiled eggs. Pour the wine dressing over the whole and decorate with olives. Serve well chilled.

SHORBA HELWAH (A Sweet-sour Sauce)
Lebanon
TO SERVE 6
1 shallot, minced
1 clove garlic, crushed
1 oz. butter
1 gill sweet red wine
1 gill bouillon
1 tablespoon sultanas
salt and pepper
1 carrot, minced
1 bay leaf
1 gill tarragon vinegar
1 gill water
1 teaspoon mint, chopped
1 teaspoon orange rind
Heat butter and cook the minced shallot and carrot with the garlic, bay leaf and seasoning for 20 minutes over a low heat. Add the wine and vinegar, water and stock and simmer for a further 25 minutes. Stir in the sultanas and orange rind, then strain through a fine sieve. Decorate with chopped mint and serve hot.

CUCUMBER SALAD

Kuwait

1 tablespoon butter
1 onion, chopped
3 teaspoons minced green pepper
2 teaspoons ginger
salt to taste
1 cup yoghurt
1 cucumber, peeled and finely chopped

MELT butter in saucepan

ADD onion, green pepper, ginger, sugar, and salt to taste. Cook over low heat until onion is tender. Remove from heat.

STIR in yoghurt and cucumber

CHILL for 1 hour

YIELD 2 to 3 servings

LIME SALAD
Saudi Arabia
TO SERVE 6

3 tablespoons gelatine
1/2 pint fresh lime juice
1 teaspoon salt
8 oz. lobster, shredded

lime sauce

1/2 pint water
3 tablespoons garlic vinegar
1/2 teaspoon white pepper
4 oz. crab, shredded

Heat water and lime juice almost to boiling point, then remove from heat. Dissolve the gelatine in the vinegar and stir into the hot juice. Allow to set partially, then rotary beat until fluffy.

Mix the lobster and crab, season and beat into the jelly. Chill until firm and serve with lime sauce.

CUCUMBER AND YOGHURT

Kuwait

1 cucumber, peeled
1/2 teaspoon salt
1 1/2 cups yoghurt
paprika
black pepper
GRATE cucumber
ADD salt. Let stand for several hours
DRAIN and press out liquid
FOLD cucumber into yoghurt
SPRINKLE with paprika and pepper
YIELD 2 to 3 servings

HERB DRESSING

Common to all Middle East countries

1 gill yoghurt
1 tablespoon parsley, finely chopped
1 tablespoon lemon juice
1 tablespoon grated horseradish
1/2 teaspoon garlic salt
6 celery leaves, finely chopped
1/2 tablespoon chives, chopped
1 tablespoon orange juice
1 tablespoon paprika pepper
1 tablespoon mint, finely chopped

Beat yoghurt a few times and add lemon and orange juice. Stir well, then add all other ingredients. Whisk for 5 minutes before serving.

SOUR CREAM FILLING

Common to all Middle East countries

3 tablespoons soft butter, unsalted
3 tablespoons sour cream
pinch salt
1 lb. sifted icing sugar
2 dessertspoons double cream
few drops peppermint essence

Cream butter and add the sifted sugar gradually. Mix until smooth, then add the creams and salt. Beat for a few minutes, then stir in the peppermint essence.

CHEESE SAUCE

Saudi Arabia

2 tablespoons plain flour
1/2 pint milk
1/2 teaspoon paprika
4 oz. grated cheese
1 tablespoon butter
1 large egg yolk
1/2 teaspoon salt

Heat butter in a saucepan, add flour and stir well. Cook for 5 minutes, stirring all the time. Add the milk gradually, taking care not to let any lumps form, and simmer for a few minutes until sauce begins to thicken.

Remove from heat, add paprika and salt and well beaten egg yolk. When this is smooth and velvety add the grated cheese.

LEBANESE SALAD

Lebanon

TO SERVE 4

1 large onion
6 spring onions
4 tomatoes
1 green pepper
4 oz. *feta* cheese
oil
wine vinegar (or lemon juice)
yoghourt
salt and pepper

Chop the onion and spring onions not too finely. Blanch, peel and de-pip the tomatoes and chop the flesh. De-stalk and de-pip the pepper and chop that. All the pieces should be of much the same size. Cut up the cheese — the Greek *feta,* though not quite the same, does very well and I know of no French or English cheese which would work — into about the same sized pieces. Put all these ingredients in a bowl and add olive oil (three parts) and vinegar or lemon juice (one part). Add a tablespoon or two of yoghourt. Season with salt and pepper. Stir gently to blend all the ingredients.

AUBERGINE SALAD

TO SERVE 4

2 aubergines
1 small onion, finely chopped
2 tablespoons olive oil
salt and pepper
juice of 1/2 lemon
1 teaspoon vinegar
lettuce leaves

Grill the aubergines so that you can skin them. Mash the pulp with all the other ingredients to make a paste. Serve on lettuce leaves, garnished with olives and slices of tomato and green pepper. It can be spread on bread or eaten with a fork.

MIXED VEGETABLE AND BREAD SALAD

1 loaf Arabic bread or 2 hard bread rolls
1 1/2 cups chopped lettuce
2/3 cup coarsely chopped onions
1 1/2 cups coarsely chopped scallions
1 cup coarsely chopped parsley
2 1/2 coarsely chopped cucumbers
2 cups coarsely chopped tomatoes
1/3 cup dried mint leaves
2 cloves garlic, crushed
1/2 cup lemon juice
2/3 cup olive oil
2 1/2 tsp salt
1/2 tsp pepper

Cut the Arabic loaf of bread open and leave it out uncovered overnight. Break the bread into small pieces and place them in a large mixing bowl. Add to it the next eight ingredients. Mix them well together and set aside to allow the bread to soften a little, about 5 minutes. Blend together the lemon juice, oil, garlic, salt and pepper and pour the dressing over the bread and vegetable mixture. Correct the seasoning adding more lemon juice if required. Mix well and serve in a large salad bowl.

BEETROOT SALAD

1 cup tahini dressing
1 cup laban (yoghurt)
1/2 lb. of diced, cooked or canned beetroots

Mix the laban with the tahini dressing and fold in the diced beetroots. Blend well and serve.

PINK SALAD

2 beetroots, boiled and mashed
2 tbs. labneh
1 1/2 cup yoghurt
5 cloves garlic, crushed
salt and pepper to taste
few green mint leaves

Blend the mashed beets, labneh, yoghurt and garlic into a smooth creamy consistency. Season with salt and pepper to taste. Serve the mixture in a deep bowl garnished with dots of labneh and whole mint leaves. The sweet and sour flavour combination is excellent and the deep pink of the salad adds colour to a table. Serve with broiled meat.

SALATET HUMMUS

Arab States

CHICK-PEAS SALAD

TO SERVE 4

6 1/2 oz. dried chick-peas
3 tablespoons finely chopped parsley, preferably flat-leaf parsley
2 oz. finely chopped onions
1/2 teaspoon finely chopped garlic
2 1/2 tablespoons fresh lemon juice
1 1/2 tablespoons olive oil
1/2 teaspoon salt
A pinch of cayenne pepper

Starting a day ahead, wash the chick-peas in a sieve under cold running water, then place them in a large bowl or pan and add enough cold water to cover them by 2 inches. Soak at room temperature for at least 12 hours. Drain the peas and place them in a small, heavy saucepan. Add enough fresh water to cover them completely and bring to the boil over a high heat. Reduce the heat to low and simmer partially covered for about 1 1/2 hours, replenishing the liquid with boiling water from time to time if necessary to keep the peas covered throughout the cooking period. When done, the peas should be tender to the bite but still somewhat firm. Drain and cool to room temperature.

MEJADDARAH

Lebanon, Syria and Palestine

2 cups large brown lentils, soaked if required
1 onion, finely chopped
Oil
Salt and black pepper
1 cup long-grain rice, washed
2 onions, sliced into half-moon shapes

Boil lentils in fresh portion of water to cover for 3/4 to 1 1/2 hours, or until tender. Fry the chopped onion in 2 tablespoons oil until soft and golden. Add it to the lentils and season to taste with salt and pepper. Mix well and add rice, together with enough water to make the liquid in the pan up to 2 cups. Season again and simmer gently, covered, for about 20 minutes until the rice is soft and well cooked, adding a little more water if it becomes absorbed too quickly.

Fry the sliced onions in 2 tablespoons very hot oil until they are dark brown and sweet, almost caramelized.

Serve the rice and lentils on a large shallow dish, garnished with fried onion slices.

This dish is delicious served either hot or cold, and accompanied by yoghurt.

RICE AND GOURDS WITH BUTTER OR OIL

Common to all Middle East countries

1 1/5 lbs. rice
3 lbs. 4 oz. gourds
6 oz. butter
7 oz. onions, chopped fine
3 tsp. salt
1/4 tsp. pepper (sweet)
2 1/4 pts. boiling water for the rice
(6 1/2 pts. for American rice)

Melt butter in a pot over medium heat, add onions and stir constantly until it browns. Add gourds which have been peeled and cut into large pieces, salt, and pepper. Stir constantly over high heat for about 5 minutes. Remove pot to moderate heat and turn its contents often. This operation requires about 30 minutes. Add boiling water to the pot and cook, high heat first, then lower heat to moderate until ingredients are cooked. Add rice which had been soaked and strained. Let boil hard for 5 minutes, then over moderate heat until rice is done. Serve hot and serve laban with it.

Note: This dish may be prepared with oil in place of butter. If cooked in oil it is then served cold.

TAHINA

Egypt

Here is the Egyptian version of Tehine (the lebanese)

8 oz. sesame paste
4 cloves garlic, crushed
4 tablespoons wine vinegar
3 tablespoons chopped parsley
1/4 pint (U.S. 2/3 cup) olive oil

Mix all the ingredients except the olive oil in a salad bowl adding, if necessary to give it a good consistency, a little hot water. Pour the olive oil round it and sprinkle some more chopped parsley on it. This is more an hors d'oeuvre dish than a dip but not much more.

TEHINE

Lebanon

garlic
salt
sesame oil
lemon juice
chopped parsley

Quantities vary, according to whether you want this as a "dip" at a cocktail party, a dip for *hors d'oeuvre* (raw carrots or cauliflower or Arab bread) or as a sauce with grilled fish — especially good with *rougets.*

Pound some cloves of garlic with salt. Add, alternately, sesame oil and lemon juice — the thick dregs of sesame oil are best — using about three parts of sesame oil to one lemon juice. Make it about as thick as thin *mayonnaise.* Stir in some chopped parsley.

LENTILS WITH RICE *mejddarah*

Lebanese style

2 cups lentils
3/4 cup rice
2 medium onions, chopped
1/2 cup olive oil
1 tsp salt
1/4 tsp cumin

Clean and wash the lentils and boil them until tender. Mash and strain them into a separate pot. Add the rice, salt and cumin and mix well.

In a pan sauté the chopped onions in oil until they turn golden brown. Add them with the oil to the lentils and rice. Bring the mixture to a boil and then simmer over a low fire for 10 minutes until the rice is cooked, stirring regularly to prevent sticking.

The lentils in this dish may also be combined with the rice unstrained or whole depending on your preference.

Mejaddarah is served lukewarm or cold with radishes, scallions, pickles or a cabbage salad.

LENTILS AND RICE *moudardara*

The ingredients are the same except that the onions should be sliced.

Clean and wash the lentils and boil them until tender. Wash the rice, drain it and add it with the salt and cumin to the lentils. Cover and cook on high heat, stirring occasionally to prevent sticking, until the lentils and rice begin to absorb the water.

Reduce the heat and simmer without further stirring until the water is absorbed completely and perforation appears. In a pan sauté the sliced onions in oil until they turn golden brown. Spread them with the oil over the lentils and rice.

Moudardara is served with Laban Cucumber, Laban Salad or Jerusaleme Salad.

TABBOULEH

CRUSHED WHEAT; TOMATO, MINT AND PARSLEY SALAD

TO SERVE 4 — 6

3 1/4 oz. fine burghul (crushed wheat)
3 medium-sized fresh, ripe tomatoes, finely chopped
3/4 oz. finely chopped parsley, preferably flat-leaf parsley
4 oz. finely chopped onions
4 tablespoons fresh lemon juice
1 1/2 teaspoons salt
4 tablespoons olive oil
1 1/2 tablespoons finely cut fresh mint or 2 1/2 teaspoons dried mint, crumbled
Cos lettuce leaves (optional)

Place the *burghul* in a bowl or pan and pour in enough cold water to cover it completely. Let it soak for about 10 minutes, then drain in a sieve or colander lined with a double thickness of dampened cheesecloth. Wrap the burghul in the cheesecloth and squeeze it vigorously until dry.

Drop the *burghul* into a deep bowl, add the tomatoes, parsley, onions, lemon juice and salt and toss gently but thoroughly together with a

fork.
Just before serving, stir in the olive oil and mint and taste for seasoning. Heap the salad in a serving bowl or spoon it on to cos lettuce leaves.

THE DISH THAT ENDS EVERYDAY FASTING DURING THE MONTH OF "RAMADAN"

FATTOUSH (Mixed Salad)

Lebanon

TO SERVE 6

3 Fresh tomatoes, medium size, cubed
2 Fresh cucumbers, peeled and diced
1 Green bell pepper, chopped fine
8 Scallions, sliced thin
4 Tablespoons parsley, chopped fine
4 Springs fresh mint, chopped fine (or creme de menthe)
1/2 Cup olive oil
1/4 Cup lemon juice
1 Teaspoon salt
2 Cups croutons

Combine and toss gently in a wooden salad bowl the tomatoes, cucumbers, green pepper, scallions, parsley and mint.

Blend olive oil, lemon juice and salt together. Add to the salad and toss lightly. Chill for 1 hour before serving. Then add croutons, toss lightly and serve on cold salad plates.

Where fresh mint is not available, a dash of creme de menthe liqueur may be used. In Damascus, some toasted bread in small pieces is added to the mixture.

Eating this dish with bread, and without the use of fork, is common all over the Arab World.

FUL MEDAMES

Egypt

This is a bean salad made with Egyptian brown beans.

TO SERVE 4 — 6

1 lb. beans
2 clove garlic
4 tablespoons olive oil
1 or 2 tablespoons lemon juice
2 teaspoons finely chopped parsley
salt and pepper

Soak the beans overnight or longer in fresh water, bring them to the boil and let them get tender — this takes about 2 1/2 hours. Let them get cold. Drain them.
Crush the garlic, add olive oil, lemon juice, chopped parsley, salt and pepper and cover the beans with this dressing. Everything depends on good olive oil, the right amount of lemon juice to supply freshness without bitterness and a nice judgement of the amount of garlic. The beans themselves are stodgy and boring: it all turns on the dressing. Some serve fresh sliced tomatoes and sliced onion with it.

HOMMOS

Chick-pea paste

Serve 6-8, costs about 28p

5 oz. chick-peas
1 large clove garlic (optional)
salt
4 — 6 tbs. Tahina (pureed sesame)
5 — 6 tbs. lemon juice
little oil
chopped parsley and paprika to garnish

Soak chick-peas in cold water overnight. Drain, cover with fresh water and boil for about 1 1/2 hours. Crush garlic with 1/4 teasp. salt. Put the Tahina, lemon juice and garlic into the liquidiser goblet, add chick-peas and blend to a creamy paste.

Turn out, add more lemon juice, and salt to taste. (It should be slightly sharp.) If you wish, add oil to give a softer texture. If you've no liquidiser, rub peas through a sieve, then beat in the garlic. Add the Tahina gradually, then lemon juice and seasoning. Turn into bowl and garnish.

VEGETABLES AND MEAT
MOULOUKHIA

TO SERVE 6 — 8

2 1/2 lbs. fresh mouloukhia, or 1 cup dried
1 1/2 lbs. veal or lamb cubes with bones on the side
1 tbs. butter
2 tsp. coriander, or 2 fresh bunches, pounded
5 gloves garlic, crushed
2 ready to cook 2 1/2 lbs. chicken
1/2 cup lemon juice
1 cup chopped onions marinated in vinegar or lemon juice
Arabic bread, toasted and pieced
salt and pepper

Stem, wash and drain the mouloukhia. With a sharp knife chop it very fine. In a cooking pot, brown the chicken and meat for 3 minutes on high heat and cover with water. Add the bones and bring the pot to a boil. Reduce the fire and simmer until the meat and chicken are done. Set them aside and reserve 1 cup of broth to use for heating them before serving.

Sauté the onions in butter and add to it the garlic and coriander. Stir over medium heat for 4 minutes. Pour over them the remainder of the chicken and meat broth. A short while before serving, add the mouloukhia to the boiling broth and cook for 3-4 minutes. Add the lemon juice and cook 2 minutes longer.

Prepare the rice according to the recipe given.

Pack it in a mold and unmold on a serving dish, and arrange the meat and chicken on top of the rice.

Serve the Mouloukhia in a deep soup bowl with the pieced toast in a separate dish.

The marinated onions are spooned over the mixture of rice, meat, mouloukhia and bread in the individual plates.

The season for the mouloukhia is spring, but it may be obtained dried in Syrian stores or gourmet shops.

RAGOUT OF COURGETTES

Lebanon

TO SERVE 4

1 lb. courgettes
salt
2 cloves garlic
4 tablespoons olive oil
8 oz. tomatoes
salt and pepper
1 tablespoon chopped parsley

Partially peel the courgettes and cut off the tops and tails. Cut them in 1/2 inch rounds. Sprinkle with salt. Chop the garlic. Skin and chop the tomatoes. Heat the oil in a heavy pan. Put in the pieces of courgettes and garlic and cook until the courgettes are soft, turning them over. Then add the tomatoes and cook to a mush. Season with salt and pepper and add the chopped parsley. Can be served hot or cold.

MACFOOL BIL CROOMBE

Morocco

TO SERVE 4 — 6

1 leek
1 tablespoon chopped chervil
2 lb. beef

salt
pinch of saffron
1/2 teaspoon cumin
pinch of cayenne
2 small or 1 medium size cabbage
1/2 pint olive oil
1 quart water
juice of 2 lemons

Pound the white part of the leek with the chervil. Put them with the beef, cut up, the salt to taste, saffron, cumin and cayenne and with the oil and water into a large saucepan. Bring to the boil and cook until the meat is quite soft — about 1 hour. Throw away the outer leaves of the cabbage or cabbages and cut the heart or hearts into medium size pieces. Poach them in salted water for about 10 minutes.

Put the beef into an ovenproof dish. On it put the pieces of cabbage. Add most of the cooking liquid. Cover with greaseproof paper and cook in the oven (375°F., Gas Mark 5) for 15 minutes. Take off the paper and cook for another 15 minutes so that the cabbage browns slightly. Squeeze on the lemon juice.

KHALTA (Aubergine with Spaghetti)

Syria, Egypt

TO SERVE 6

3 large aubergines
1 lb. cooked spaghetti
1/4 pint bouillon made from cube
6 oz. toasted brown breadcrumbs
2 heaped tablespoons flour
3 tablespoons butter
2 green peppers, thinly sliced
1 lb. tomatoes, skinned and chopped
6 oz. grated cheese
1/4 pint yoghurt
salt and pepper

Put the spaghetti in a well buttered baking dish, add the tomatoes and green peppers in layers and sprinkle each layer with a little seasoning and flour. Cover with the aubergines, cut lengthwise in quarters and well cleaned so that no bitterness remains.

Add bouillons to yoghurt and beat a few times with a fork so that the two are well combined, and pour over vegetables and spaghetti. Sprinkle with the cheese and breadcrumbs and dot with butter. Bake for 60-70 minutes in hot oven, 350°F. — Regulo 3, and serve hot.

RICE AND SPINACH

Lebanon

olive oil
1 onion
1 lb. spinach
water
salt and pepper
4 oz. rice, cooked

Heat the oil in a pan. Chop the onion finely and toss in it the oil till it is golden. Wash the spinach and add it, undried, and stir it about for 10 minutes by which time it should be soft. Add a little more boiling water. Season. Stir in the rice and cook it over a low flame so that the water is absorbed. Let it get cold.

BAMYA

Common to all Middle East countries

TO SERVE 6

2 lb. okra
2 large tomatoes chopped
1 tablespoon mint, chopped
1/2 oz. butter
1/4 pint bone stock
2 large onions, chopped finely
1 tablespoon parsley, chopped
1 tablespoon dill, chopped
1 lemon juice
ground black pepper,
salt to taste

Wash okra and cut off stems carefully so that pods will not burst in cooking. Put in a bowl and mix with the lemon juice. Leave aside for 30 minutes.

Cook the onion in butter for 5 minutes, add tomatoes, parsley, herbs and seasoning. Bring to boil and simmer for 10 minutes.

Drain okra and put into a casserole. Pour the onion mixture over, cover tightly and simmer for 2 hours.

BAZILLA (Peas with Lamb)

TO SERVE 6

2 lb. shelled peas
2 tablespoons dill, chopped
1 1/2 pints marrow bone stock
2 onions, chopped
1/2 tablespoon brown sugar
1 lb. boned lamb
1/2 teaspoon fresh thyme, chopped
4 tablespoons clarified fat
1 teaspoon sorrel leaves, chopped
1/2 teaspoon celery salt

Cut meat into small pieces. Melt fat, add onions, meat, thyme, sorrel, half the dill, and seasoning. Cover and cook for 30 minutes over moderate heat, shaking pan frequently to prevent burning. Add stock and bring to boil slowly, skimming as necessary. Add sugar and peas and simmer for 40 minutes, or until peas are tender but not "mushy". In the case of very young fresh peas the cooking time will be considerably reduced, so test with a fork.

Add rest of dill, stir once and remove from heat. Serve in own juices.

EGGPLANT CASSEROLE

Bedingan Masri — *Egypt*

2 onions, chopped
1/4 cup butter
1 pound beef, ground
1 cup water
1 can (6 ounces) tomato paste
1 teaspoon salt
1/4 teaspoon black pepper
1 large eggplant
shortening (for browning)
SAUTÉ onions in butter in skillet until tender
1 teaspoon ground ginger root
1 teaspoon paprika
1 teaspoon curry powder
1/4 teaspoon garlic salt
1/2 teaspoon turmeric
1 inch cinnamon stick

Vegetables and Fruits

2 bay leaves
3 cups cooked drained vegetables,
(potatoes, cauliflower, peas, or other vegetables, or a combination)
salt (to taste)
BROWN onions in oil in skillet
ADD seasonings. Cook for 3 minutes. Remove

whole spices
ADD vegetables, and salt to taste
REHEAT
YIELD 1 to 6 servings

TAHINAT EL BEID

Lebanon

2 tablespoons sesame oil
lemon juice
water
1 clove garlic, crushed
1 tablespoon chopped parsley
salt
1 hard-boiled egg

Put the oil in a salad bowl and add lemon juice drop by drop — the quantity depends on how astringent you want it. Thin with a little water. Add the garlic, parsley and salt and the egg very finely chopped. Sprinkle on cayenne.

This is another bread dip.

DAMASCUS ARTICHOKES

TO SERVE 4

3 small globe artichokes
1 gill olive oil
1 teaspoon coriander seeds
1 gill mayonnaise No. 2
1/2 pint dry cider
1 lemon juice
pinch of nutmeg
salt and pepper

Clean and pare the artichokes and remove outer, lower leaves. Cut off thorny leaf tips. Put into hot cider, to which 1 teaspoon lemon juice has been added and parboil for 10 minutes. Drain.

Strain the cider and return to saucepan, add olive oil, rest of lemon juice, coriander seeds, nutmeg and seasoning and bring to boil slowly. Add the parboiled artichokes and cook for another 20 minutes, increasing the heat slightly. Remove artichokes, drain and allow to cool. Strain liquor and allow to cool. When quite cold add the mayonnaise and whisk for 5 minutes. Spoon this mixture over the cold artichokes, chill for 1 hour and then serve.

MAGHREBIA

The basic process for the preparation of *MAGHREBIA* is the steaming of the grain over a stew or broth. This is generally made with meat, usually lamb or chicken, and a variety of vegetables. Chick-peas are usually added, and sometimes raisins as well. Many spices are used but so sparingly that one can hardly define each individual aroma. Often a sauce is prepared separately with some of the broth and made strong and fiery with cayenne or chili pepper. This sauce is served beside the *MAGHREBIA* for those who wish to be "inflamed and intoxicated".

The actual process of cooking the *MAGHREBIA* is very simple, but calls for a subtle handling of the grain. The aim is to make it swell and become extremely light, each grain soft, delicate, velvety, and separate from its neighbor. The grain must never cook in the broth or sauce, but only in the steam. It must not even touch the broth throughout the steaming.

It is as easy as this: Steam the *MAGHREBIA* over boiling water, and then serve it with a stew prepared separately.

(MOUGHRABIA)

Lebanon

TO SERVE 6 — 8

1 lb. kous-kous (may be obtained in gourmet stores in a dried form)
3 lbs. frying chicken, diced
1 lb. beef or lamb, cubes with bones on the side
2 tsp. butter
2 tsp. salt
1/2 tsp powdered caraway seeds
1/2 tsp. cinnamon
1/4 tsp. pepper
10 small onions
1 can chick-peas, or 1 cup dried, soak overnight
1 carrot, sliced
1 large onion, quartered
2 bay leaves
2 springs of parsley

To prepare the Kous-Kous, drop the carrot, onion, bay leaves and parsley in enough water in a large cooking pot to steam for 1 hour. Place a fitting sieve over the pot and put the Kous-Kous in it. Paste together the edges of the sieve and the pot along their circumferences to prevent the steam from escaping. Dough may be used for this purpose. Cover the sieve with a thick cloth. Steam the Kous-Kous for 1 hour. This long process may be omitted if the Kous-Kous is fresh and not fried.

Meanwhile, cover the chicken and meat with water and bring it to a boil, uncovered. Add the bay leaf, cinnamon, salt and pepper. Skim the stock until it is clear of grease. Remove the meat and chicken to a side dish. Reserve a small quantity of the stock.

Sauté the onions in butter and add them to the meat stock in the cooking pot. Bring to a boil and simmer for 5 minutes. Add the chick-peas and Kous-Kous and bring to a boil once again. Add the caraway seeds, season and simmer for 15 minutes or until the Kous-Kous is done. Add the sautéeing butter and simmer a little longer until the gravy forms on the side.

Serve the Kous-Kous in a large tray topped with the pieces of chicken and meat with the remaining gravy on the side.

Although this dish requires time and effort, the final result is very gratifying. It is a truly exotic dish which presents beautifully at a buffet dinner.

KUSKUSI

Egypt

2 lb. 4 oz. flour

water

Over half the flour in a wooden dish sprinkle 2 tablespoons of water, and work it well, rubbing continually between the hands. Continue adding a small handful of flour and a sprinkling of water until all the flour is in use. Take out the larger lumps now and again to be worked apart, and, when broken up, to be thrown back among the rest. Work in this way for 20 minutes or longer, adding no more water and rubbing between the hands until the whole is in grains resembling large semolina in appearance. Put through a sieve to ensure uniformity in size, and leave to dry. Cook as directed in recipe.

If kuskusi cannot be made at home nor obtained ready made, then semolina, though smaller, may be used as a substitute.

BABA GHANOUSH (Eggplant with Tahini)

This rich cream is a combination of two strong flavors: the smoky one of eggplants prepared as below, and the strong taste of tahini sharpened by lemon and garlic. It is exciting and vulgarly seductive. The ingredients are added almost entirely to taste, the harmony of flavors depending largely on the size and flavor of the egg-plant used.

The quantities below give a fairly large amount, enough to be served as a dip at a party.

3 large eggplants
2-4 cloves garlic, or to taste
Salt
1/2 cup tahini or less,
depending on the size of the eggplants
juice of 3 lemons, or more to taste
1/2 teaspoon ground cumin (optional)

2 tablespoons finely chopped parsley
A few black olives or 1 tomato, thinly sliced, to garnish

Cook the eggplants over charcoal or under a gas or electric broiler as described in the recipe for eggplant puree, until the skin blackens and blister. Peel and wash the eggplants, and squeeze out as much of the bitter juice as possible.

Crush the garlic cloves with salt. Mash the eggplants with a potato masher or fork, then add the crushed garlic and a little more salt, and pound to a smooth, creamy puree. Alternatively, use an electric blender to make the puree.

Add the *tahini* and lemon juice alternately, beating well or blending for a few seconds between each addition. Taste and add more salt, lemon juice, garlic, or *tahini* if you think it necessary, and if you like, a little cumin.

Pour the cream into a bowl or a few smaller serving dishes. Garnish with finely chopped parsley and black olives, or with a few tomato slices. Serve as an appetizer with Arab or other bread, as a salad, or as a party dip.

RAGOUT OF TOMATOES WITH MEAT

Lebanon

5 1/2 lbs. ripe tomatoes, peeled, cut into large pieces and seed removed
1 lb. 1 1/2 oz. meat
5 oz. butter
2 oz. snobar (pine nuts)
1 1/2 oz. garlic, chopped fine
3 1/2 oz. onions, chopped fine
2 1/2 tsp. salt
1/3 tsp. pepper

Heat butter in a pot and fry onions, garlic and meat. Add snobar. Stir and turn well. Add tomatoes, salt and pepper. Cook over moderate heat until done. Rice cooked, is served with this dish.

LOUBIA

Algeria

TO SERVE 4 — 6

1 lb. haricot beans
salt
4 cloves garlic
2 pinches of cumin
3 pinches of paprika
2 cloves, pounded
1 pinch of cayenne pepper
2 tablespoons olive oil

Soak the beans overnight. Cook them in salted water until they are done but still firm. While they are cooking, pound the garlic in a mortar and add the cumin, paprika, cloves and cayenne. Mix in the olive oil. When the beans are cooked, drain off the water and add the sauce. Cook just to heat through. It makes a very good accompaniment to roast lamb.

Sample illuminated pages from a Quran which dates to the eighteenth century.

EGGPLANT AND RICE

Mecca — Saudi Arabia

1 dash Tabasco
1/2 teaspoon mustard seeds
1/2 teaspoon cumin seed
1 teaspoon poppy seeds
1/2 teaspoon turmeric
4 peppercorns

- 3 whole cloves
- 1 teaspoon cinnamon
- 2 tablespoons peanuts
- 6 tablespoons butter
- 1 eggplant cut in 1/2 inch cubes
- 1 onion, finely chopped
- 4 cups cooked rice
- 1 cup flaked coconut

GRIND and blend hot pepper sauce, mustard seeds, cumin seed, poppy seeds, turmeric, peppercorns, olives, cinnamon, and peanuts

MELT 1 tablespoon butter. Cook blended spices in butte: for 1 minute

RUB eggplant slices with spice mixture

MELT 2 tablespoons butter in large skillet. Add onion and cook until lightly browned on both sides, 6 to 8 minutes

MELT 3 tablespoons butter in separate pan. Add rice and fry well

ARRANCE eggplant and rice in serving dish

GARNISH with coconut

WARAQ DAWALI MAHSHI
(Vine Leaves Stuffed with Meat)

Common to all Middle East countries

TO SERVE 6

1 lb. vine leaves
2 onions (chopped)
6 springs dill
4 oz. mushrooms, sliced
garlic salt
2 oz. rice
1 lb. lamb, minced
1/2 teaspoon rosemary leaves
1/2 pint sweet white wine
4 tablespoons clarified fat
1/2 teaspoon white pepper

Put the washed and cleaned vine leaves into boiling water and cook for 5 minutes. Strain, cut off stalks and cut each leaf in half down the middle vein.

Melt half the fat and lightly brown onions, add mushrooms and cook another 5 minutes. Add stock, the cleaned rice, and cook for 12 minutes on moderate heat until all liquid has been absorbed by the rice. Remove from heat, add lamb, dill, rosemary leaves and seasoning and knead for 5 minutes.

With the hairy sides of the leaves facing upwards put 1 heaped teaspoon of stuffing on each leaf and roll up fairly tightly, shiny sides of leaves facing outwards.

Arrange side by side at bottom of a shallow pan, layer by layer, and add rest of clarified fat and the wine. Cover with a plate with a heavy weight on top, put lid on pan and cook over moderate heat for 35 minutes. Serve hot in own juices.

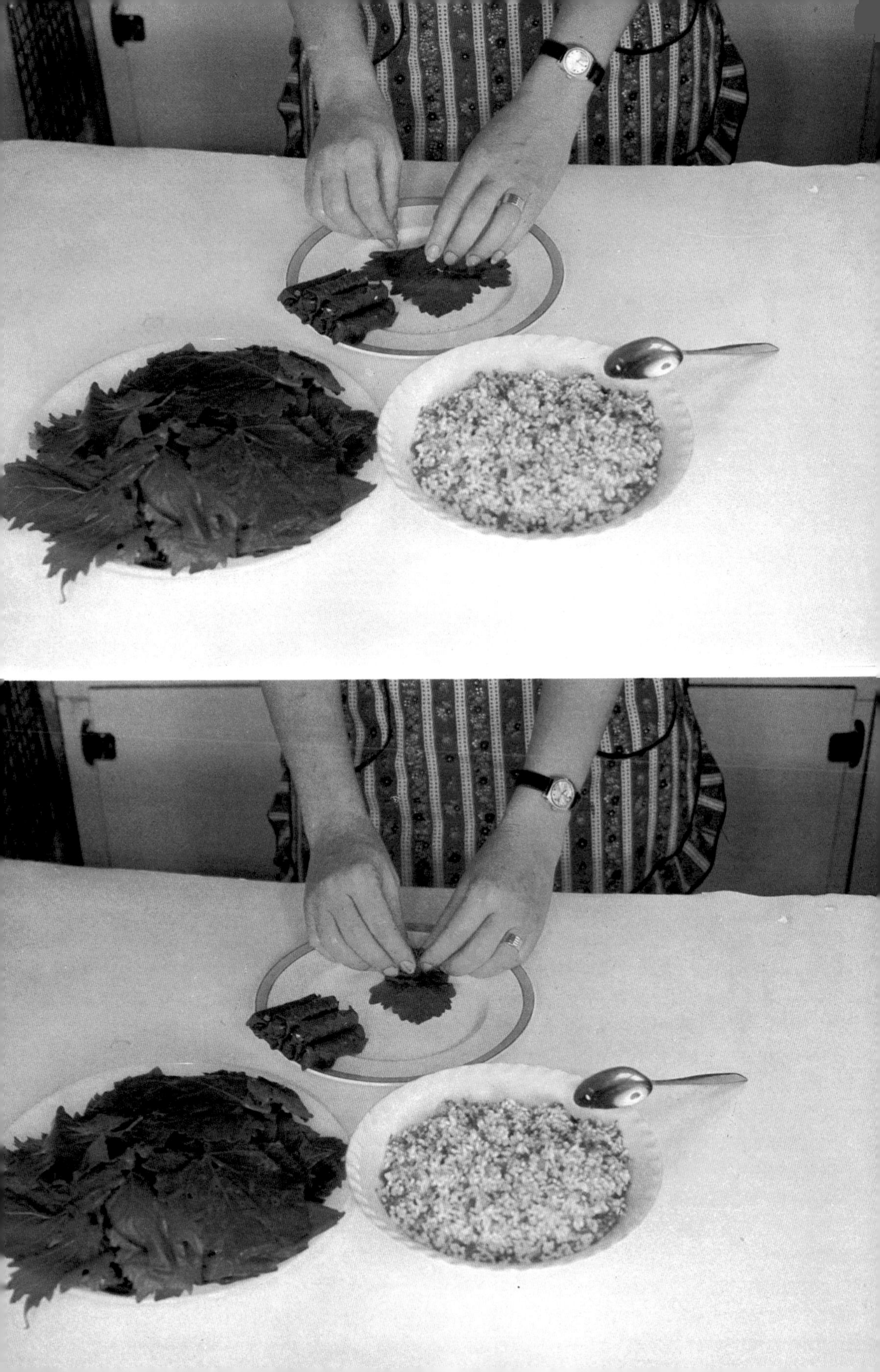

MALFOOF MAHSHI
(Cabbage Stuffed with Meat)

Common to all Middle East countries

TO SERVE 6

1 1/2 lb. white cabbage
1 lb. minced beef
4 tablespoons clarified fat
3 onions, finely chopped
salt and pepper
1/4 pint water, boiling
3 oz. Patna rice
1 tablespoon tomato ketchup
1/4 pint bouillon (from cube)

Cut cabbage in half, lengthwise, and take out the tender middle part (this can be used, grated, for salads). Wash remaining cabbage and put into boiling salted water and cook for 3 minutes. Strain off water and allow cabbage to cool.

Tear off leaves gently and cut into 4-inch squares. Melt half the fat, add onions and fry until a pale brown. Add cleaned rice and bouillon and cook over moderate heat until rice is tender — about 10 to 1 minutes. Remove from heat, add meat and seasoning and combine thoroughly.

Take 1 teaspoon of this mixture and place on centre of a square of cabbage leaf, fold envelope fashion and arrange at bottom of a shallow, wide-based pan. Continue in this way until all cabbage and filling have been used. Add tomato ketchup and rest of fat and pour on the boiling water. Cover pan with a plate with a heavy weight and cook for 35 minutes on very moderate heat.
Serve hot.

BEDINJAN MAHSHI (Stuffed Sliced Eggplant)

Syria and Lebanon

1 large eggplant
1/2 cup oil
1/2 cup minced onion
1 garlic clove, minced
1/2 pound lean, lamb or beef, ground
2 eggs, beaten
2 tablespoons chopped parsley
2 cups soft bread crumbs
1 teaspoon cinnamon
1 teaspoon salt
1/4 teaspoon black pepper

PARE eggplant; cut in 8 uniform lengthwise slices
FRY in oil until almost cooked but still firm
RESERVE oil
SAUTÉ onion and garlic in 1 tablespoon of reserved oil until tender
ADD meat. Cook, stirring, until browned
MIX in remaining ingredients
SPREAD stuffing between each 2 slices eggplant
FASTEN with picks
PLACE in a shallow baking pan
POUR remaining oil over all
BAKE at 350°F for 30 minutes

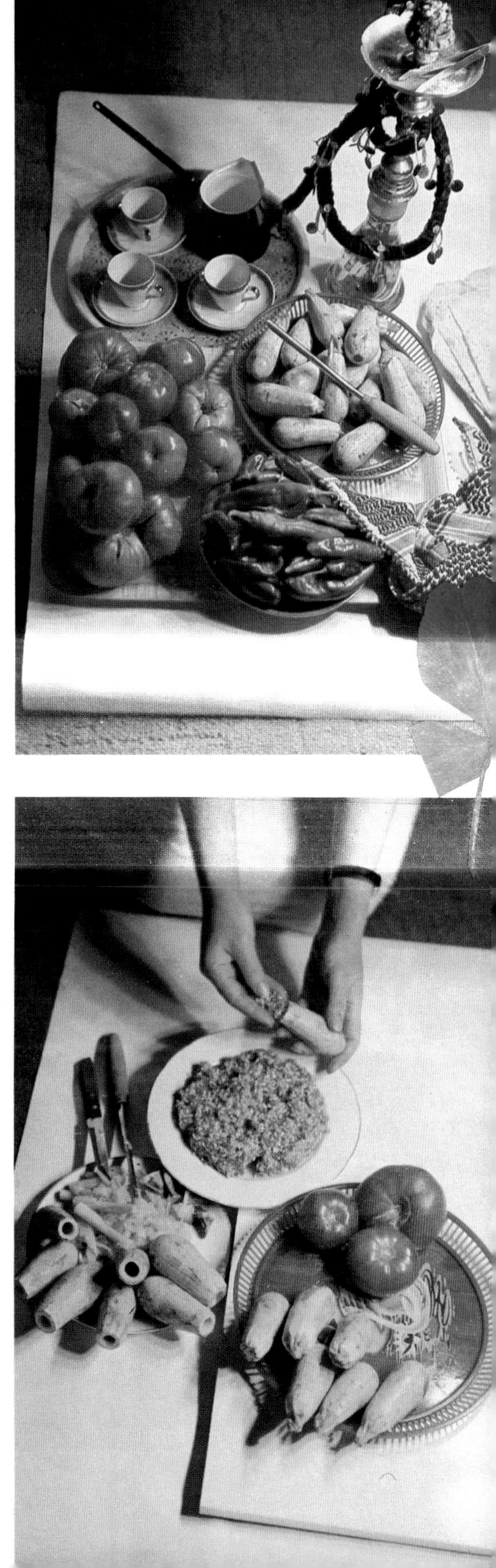

Stuff the vegetables with either filling, moistening with a little extra olive oil. Cover with the reserved tops. Arrange the stuffed vegetables in one layer in a wide baking dish into which you have poured a few tablespoons of oil. Chop the tomato pulp, add about 1/2 cup water, season with a little salt and pepper, and pour over the vegetables. Add enough extra to come halfway up to the vegetable.

Cover the dish with a lid or a sheet of foil, and bake in a preheated moderate oven (375°F) or 40 minutes; then uncover, add a little more water if it has all been absorbed, and bake for a further 20 minutes, or until the vegetables are colored and well done.

Serve hot or cold as a first course, or hot as a main dish, accompanied by various salads and rice.

In the past, it was usual to deep-fry or sauté the vegetables before stewing them gently in a sauce or baking them in a slow oven. Today, this is still done by some cooks who prefer the richer taste. You can also cook the vegetables on top of the stove. Arrange them in a large heavy pan, half-cover with water mixed with a few tablespoons of oil, and simmer, covered, for about 1 hour over very low heat, adding water if necessary, a little at a time. Sprinkle with a little lemon juice towards the end of cooking. In this case, the filling need not be precooked, but do not fill the vegetables too tightly to allow room for the rice to expand.

STUFFED KIBBEH

Syrian

This is the most popular as well as the most intriguing of *kibbeh.* The preparation of these small *kibbeh* requires all the talent of *kibbeh* making. Syrian women measure their art and make their reputations by their craftsmanship and finesse when making this dish. The art lies in making the outer shells as long, as thin, and as even as possible. The crisp, light, tasty shells should crack to divulge a juicy, aromatic meat filling.

Prepare the *kibbeh* meat mixture as for raw *kibbeh* using 1 lb. meat to 2 cups burghul, and the filling as for *kibbeh bil sanieh* (above).

Wet your hands with cold water. Take a small lump of *kibbeh* mixture the size of an egg. Holding it in your left hand, make a hole in it with a finger of the right hand and use the left hand to pat the paste around the finger and work it into a long, slim, oval shape, pressing it up the finger, widening it and slipping it around and around. This is rather reminiscent of pottery making. If the paste cracks, dip a finger in cold water and use it to stick the shell together again. There must be no holes in the shell. British soldiers in the Middle East during the Second World War used to call these *kibbeh* Syrian torpedos, and I think that this describes their shape rather well.

Fill the shell with about a tablespoon of filling. Close the opening by wetting the rim with cold water and sticking the edges together. Pat and smooth into a thin end to achieve a slim, oval shape. If you find all this too difficult, make a small round or oval shape. This seems easier to achieve.

Deep-fry the torpedos in oil to a rich, dark brown color. Drain. Serve hot or cold with a selection of salads: ground almond, a *tahina* cream salad or a mixed fresh vegetable salad.

These *kibbeh* can be prepared ahead and fried just before serving, or fried and warmed up again in a covered dish in the oven. Smaller versions are cooked for the last 1/2 hour in egg-plant, zucchini, and meat stews.

Left: Kibbeh with sauce. *Above. Kibbeh without sauce.*

KIBBEH BISSONIYYAH
(Fried Stuffed Minced Lamb Patties)
Lebanon — Syria — Jordan
TO SERVE 6

Stuffing

1 1/2 tablespoons olive oil
1 1/2 tablespoons pine kernels
1 1/2 tablespoons finely chopped onions
4 oz. lean boneless lamb,
preferably leg of lamb, coarsely minced
1/8 teaspoon ground allspice
1/2 teaspoon salt

First layer Kibbeh

Second layer stuffing *(page 169)*

Third layer Kibbeh

Freshly ground black pepper
(Patties: Kibbeh Nayya with 3/8 pint olive oil)
Make the stuffing in the following way: Heat the 1 tablespoon of olive oil in a heavy, medium-size frying pan, over a moderate heat until a light haze forms above it. Drop in the pine kernels and brown them lightly.
Transfer the nuts to a plate with a perforated spoon. Add the onions to the oil remaining in the frying pan and cook for about 5 minutes, stirring constantly, until they are soft and transparent but not brown. Add the lamb and cook until all traces of pink disappear, mashing it frequently with the back of a spoon to break up any lumps. Tip the pan and drain off any excess fat. Stir the pine kernels, allspice, salt and a few grindings of pepper into the lamb mixture, taste for seasoning and set aside off the heat.

Divide the KIBBEH NAYYA into 6 equal portions and, moistening your hands with cold water from time to time, roll them into egg-shaped patties about 4 inches long and 2 1/2 inches in diameter in the middle. Make a tunnel-like pocket about 3 inches deep and 1 inch across lengthway into each patty with your forefinger, starting from one of the tapered ends. Gently

press about 1 1/2 tablespoons of the stuffing mixture into each pocket and, dipping your hands in cold water, reshape the patty around the stuffing to enclose it completely. Heat the olive oil over a high heat in a large, heavy frying pan until a light haze forms above it. Add the stuffed lamb patties and fry them for about 15 minutes, turning them occasionally with a spoon and regulating the heat so that they brown evenly on all sides without burning. The patties are done when the lamb shows no trace of pink when pierced gently with the point of a sharp knife.

STUFFED POTATOES

Lebanon

12 largish potatoes
4 tablespoons butter
Filling, including pine nuts, if you like, raisins
4 tablespoons tomato paste
Salt and black pepper
6 tablespoons oil

Choose a type of potato which does not disintegrate easily. Peel the tomatoes and hollow them out with an apple corer or a small pointed knife. Turn them in hot butter for a few minutes until they are slightly colored.

Prepare the filling. Stuff the potatoes with it and pack them tightly side by side in a large over dish. Dilute the tomato paste with enough water to half-cover the potatoes. Season to taste with salt, pepper, add oil, and mix well. Pour over the potatoes.

Bake, uncovered, in a preheated moderate oven (375°F) until the potatoes have browned a little. Then cover with a lid, and continue to bake for 3/4 hour longer, or until the potatoes are soft but do not fall apart, and most of the sauce has been absorbed.

BASAL MAHSHI

Lebanon (Stuffed Onions)
Common to most Middle East countries

TO SERVE 4

4 large onions
4 oz. buttered white crumbs
4 springs parsley
4 oz. cooked minced veal
1 gill double cream
salt and pepper

Peel onions and cook in boiling salted water until fairly tender, for about 15 minutes. Drain and cool. Cut thin slices from root ends, hollow out centres carefully but leave an outer shell about 1/2 inch in thickness. Chop centres very finely and mix with the veal, cream, 2 table-spoons bread crumbs and seasoning. Fill onions shells with this mixture.

Lay onions side by side in a shallow well-buttered baking dish, top with remaining crumbs, dot with butter and bake for 1 hour at 350°F. — Regulo 3. Serve hot decorated with a spring of parsley to each onion.

STUFFED CARROTS

12 large carrots (6 inches long and 1 inch diameter)
1 medium onion, chopped
1 lb minced lamb or beef
1 tbs butter
2 tbs pine seeds
1 cup consomme or beef broth

Prepare the carrots for stuffing by removing a thin slice from the bottom and scraping the inside pulp out thereby hollowing the carrot and leaving the cone-like end uncut.

To prepare the filling, stir the onions into the butter in a pan until they are lightly browned. Add the meat and stir occasionally until the meat sears well. Season with salt and pepper to taste. Add boiling water and cook well.

Sauté the pine seeds and mix them well with the cooked meat. Stuff the carrots with the filling and brown them in butter until they are softened. Arrange them in an oven-proof casserole. Season with salt and pepper to taste. Add enough beef broth to cover a good part of the carrots. Cover the casserole and place it in a 350°F oven. Add more broth if necessary. When the carrots are tender and well cooked, strain the liquid and

thicken it with flour blended to a paste with lemon juice. Pour the lemon sauce over the carrots and simmer for about 1/2 hour.
Serve with mashed potatoes or rice.

STUFFED BAKED EGGPLANT

Batinjan bil saneeyee or sheikh il mahshi
TO SERVE 6
3 eggplants
1 12-oz. can tomato puree
Skin eggplant. Cut in quarters lengthwise. Sauté in butter. Place side by side in baking tray. Slit pieces in centre and stuff each piece with 1 tablespoon stuffing. Pour tomato puree (thinned with a little water) over the eggplant. Bake in moderately hot oven (350°F) for 20 minutes.

STUFFING (Hashwa)
1 pound ground lamb
1/2 pound butter
1/2 onion, chopped
1 cup pine nuts
Dash of allspice, nutmeg, and cinnamon
Salt and pepper to taste

KABAB MAHSHI (Stuffed Marrows)

Common to most Middle East countries

TO SERVE 6

3 marrows
1 teaspoon sweet marjoram
3 oz. Patna rice
1 teaspoon white pepper
2 tablespoons parsley, finely chopped
salt to taste
juice of half lemon
1 lb. lamb (without fat), minced
3 tomatoes, skinned and seeded
1 teaspoon chervil, finely chopped
3 tablespoons clarified fat
1 large onion, finely chopped
1 gill dry white wine

Select fat young marrows. Cut off the bottom end. Scoop out inside, throw away seeds, cover marrows with water and lemon juice and leave aside.

Heat half the fat and fry onions until transparent but not brown. Add wine and the washed and well dried rice.

STUFFED AUBERGINES WITH RAGOUT

Lebanon

TO SERVE 6—8

1 lb. aubergines
salt
4 oz. lean meat
2 oz. butter
4 oz. rice, boiled and dried
salt and pepper
1/4 teaspoon saffron
8 oz. tomatoes
2 oz. butter
ragout of aubergine with meat
boiling water

Cut the aubergines in half and scoop out some of the flesh. Salt them and leave them to drain, open side downwards, on a sieve for 30 minutes. Chop the meat and toss it in butter. Stir in the cooked rice, the salt, pepper and saffron, and stuff the half aubergines with this mixture. Peel and chop the tomatoes and cook them to a puree in butter.

Line a flameproof dish with the ragout of aubergine. On it arrange the stuffed aubergines.

Cover them with the tomato puree. Add a lit
boiling water — you must not make it runny (a
you can always add more, if need be) — and co
on a brisk flame. When it is bubbling, turn do
the heat and cook till the aubergine flesh is s
— 20-30 minutes.

Serve hot in the dish in which it has cooked.

EGGS

BEID BEJEBN (Eggs with Cheese)

Damascus

TO SERVE 4

4 oz. grated Parmesan cheese
1 teaspoon dry mustard
4 tablespoons gherkins, finely chopped
1/2 pint Yeshil Salcha
salt and pepper
4 hard-boiled eggs
1 teaspoon grated horseradish
12 asparagus tips, cooked
1 dessertspoon poppy seed

Arrange the washed and dried cos lettuce leaves on a serving dish and sprinkle with the cheese.

Slice eggs in half, remove yolks and put through a sieve. Mix this with seasoning, dry mustard, poppy seeds, gherkins and borseradish, moisten with a little Yeshil Salcha and fill the egg whites. Arrange these, stuffed side downwards, on the cheese. Spoon over the whole the rest of the Yeshil Salcha and strew the top with the asparagus tips. Serve cold.

FRIED EGGS WITH BEEF AND ONION

Lebanon

Ingredients: TO SERVE 4

200 g (12 oz.) ground beef
8 eggs
6 tablespoon oil
dash of pepper
1/2 tablespoon sugar
1 tablespoon salt
1 onion

Mix the eight eggs. Add sugar and salt. Cut the onion to 1 cm pieces and mix with the ground beef. Fry it to desired. Heat 1 1/2 tablespoon oil. Fry 1/4 of the egg mixture until the down side is light brown. Spread 1/4 of the ground beef mixture with onion. Fold the frying eggs in half engulfing the beef. Fry the upper side of the eggs until light brown.

Repeat this for four times. Serve one piece to each person.

STUFFED OMELET
Medina

Saudi Arabia

Because of Medina's very warm climate, the diet is light, though spicy.

2 garlic cloves, thinly sliced
3 tablespoons oil
1/2 pound meat ground
20 peanuts, minced
1/2 cup thinly sliced onions
2 teaspoons sugar
1 1/2 tablespoons soy sauce
1/8 teaspoon black pepper
6 eggs, beaten

Garlic in oil in skillet

ADD butter and nuts. Cook for 10 minutes, stirring frequently

STIR in onions, sugar, soy sauce, and pepper. Cook for 2 minutes. Reserve

COOK eggs in oil in skillet making 2 large cakes

PLACE half the filling on each cake

FOLD in half and serve

YIELD 2 cakes

SUGGESTED MENU: Stuffed Omelet, mashed potatoes, coffee or tea.

STUFFED EGGS BEYTH MAHSHI

Saudi Arabia

TO SERVE 6

6 hard-boiled eggs
1 teaspoon honey
6 oz. cooked spinach
1/2 pint herb dressing
1 tablespoon yoghurt
1 teaspoon olive oil
1 teaspoon French mustard
salt and pepper

Cut a slice from pointed end of each egg and remove the yolks, taking care not to break the whites.

Sieve the yolks and put in a bowl with the yoghurt, sherry, olive oil, mustard and seasoning. Mix well together, then fill the whites with mixture. Stand eggs upright on a bed of spinach and add herb dressing. Chill for 1 hour before serving.

EGG KABAB (Aijet Beythat)

Saudi Arabia

8 hard-cooked eggs, shelled
1/4 cup butter
3/3 teaspoon salt
3/4 teaspoon paprika
3/4 teaspoon white pepper
3/4 teaspoon cinnamon

PRICK whites of eggs all over so they won't split as they are heated through

SAUTÉ eggs in butter over low heat, turning, until light brown

MIX seasonings. Sprinkle over eggs

YIELD 4 to 8 servings

Stuffed sheep or cow guts boiled half done

To be covered with butter

Fried to taste

STUFFED SHEEP GUTS WITH TOMATO RAGOUT

Lebanon

Ingredients:

4 guts
1 lb. meat with some fat, ground or cut fine
6 oz. rice
2 tbs. salt
1/2 tsp. white pepper
1/8 tsp. saffron
1 lb. meat cut in pieces for the ragout
1 oz. cold water
8 oz. butter (to fry guts)
4 1/2 lbs. ripe tomatoes for ragout
1 1/2 tbs. salt
1/2 tsp. spices
1 pt. water
5 oz. butter
8 oz. small onions, peeled and left whole
3 oz. chopped onions

Guts are cleaned. Mix stuffing of ground meat, rice, some of the salt and spices and the small, whole onions. Boil and remove skin. Boil half done. Remove from pot and fry in hot butter and add to tomato ragout which has been prepared. Cook together until all is done. Serve each of these dishes in a separate container.

HEAD AND FEET OF SHEEP WITH LABAN AND TOASTED BREAD

Ingredients:

Head of one sheep and 8 feet
6 oz. laban strained in a sack for 45 minutes
2 tbs. salt
5 cloves garlic
1 1/2 oz. butter
1 1/2 lb. toasted Arab bread
1 oz. pine nuts (snobar), dried mint and red pepper for garnishing

Prepare and cook head and feet.

Mash garlic with salt and mix it with the laban and add dry mint. Ten minutes before it is time to serve, remove meat from the head and feet. Crumble the toasted bread and spread it in a deep, wide platter or tray and sprinkle it with some of the broth in which head was cooked. Cover it with the meat from the head and feet. Pour the laban mixture over it and sprinkle more dry mint and red pepper. Pine nuts which had been roasted in melted butter may be added as the last touch.

KHAROUF MAHSHOU

Lamb with stuffing

SERVES 8

3 lb. shoulder of lamb
6 oz. butter or oil
1 lb. long grain rice
1 lb. minced lamb
seasoning and spices
1/2 oz. almonds
1/2 oz. pine nuts
1/2 oz. pistachio nuts
parsley.

Cut the lamb into large pieces and fry in a little of the oil. Put into a casserole, cover with water and boil for about 1 hour.

Fry minced lamb for 10 minutes in a little more of the oil, stir in rice, seasoning and spices. Then stir in 1/2 pint stock from meat. Cook for about 20 minutes. Meanwhile, fry nuts in rest of oil. Put lamb in a deep serving dish. Cover with rice, pressing down well, nuts and parsley. Use remaining stock for gravy.

AKLET SULTAN (Sultan's Meal)

Damascus

TO SERVE 6

6 eggs
6 chicken livers
2 tablespoons Madeira
1/4 pint double cream, soured
salt and pepper
butter
6 tomatoes
1 clove crushed garlic
2 tablespoons parsley, finely chopped
6 oz. buttered white breadcrumbs
2 tablespoons hot olive oil

Cut tomatoes in half and put them in a pan, cut side down, with the hot olive oil sprinkled over them. Cook for 1 minute, then turn on other side and cook for another minute. Sprinkle with the breadcrumbs, garlic and parsley. Cook for 1 minute more, then remove from heat.

Butter a flat baking dish and break in the eggs, one by one. Dot with butter, season and cook at 350°F. — Regulo 3, for 10 minutes, basting yolks now and then with the hot butter.

Arrange the eggs on a hot serving dish, surround with the tomato mixture. Sauté the chicken livers in Madeira for 3 minutes over a fierce heat and place on top of the tomatoes. Whisk the sour cream and pour round edge of dish. Serve at once.

FRIED BRAIN OMELETTE

Lebanon

Ingredients:

5 brains of lamb or
2 brains of beef
1 1/2 tbs. salt
1/2 tsp. white pepper
3 tbs. flour
11 oz. butter
6 eggs

Boil brains. Cool and cut into rounded pieces and sprinkle with salt and pepper. Break eggs and separate white from yellows. Put egg whites in a deep bowl and beat till it forms thick foam. Add to it the beaten egg yellow. Beat again after adding salt and pepper. Add flour and turn lightly with a spoon. Melt butter in skillet. Dip pieces of brains into the beaten eggs and lift the pieces with a spoon taking some of the eggs with it and drop this into the hot butter. Keep the fried brains warm in a container near the heat until ready to serve. Serve with it vegetables or potatoes.

(Lamb in Greaseproof Paper)

Damascus

TO SERVE 6

2 lb. top part leg lamb
2 tomatoes, skinned
2 carrots, diced small
2 tablespoons clarified fat
2 tablespoons thyme, chopped
1 teaspoon garlic salt
8 oz. butter for frying
2 chopped onions
2 tablespoons dill, chopped
6 oz. cooked green peas
1 gill dry white wine
3 potatoes, cut in thin rounds
1/2 teaspoon freshly ground white pepper
greaseproof paper

MOARRAQ

Saudi Arabia

TO SERVE 6

1 lb. lamb, diced
1 clove crushed garlic
3 tablespoons parsley, chopped
2 teaspoons cayenne pepper
7 oz. Patna rice
3/4 pint boiling water
4 tablespoons olive oil
1 red pepper, finely chopped
1 teaspoon salt
3 shallots, finely chopped
6 black olives

Heat the oil and cook the shallots for 3 minutes. Add the garlic, meat, red pepper and seasoning and cook for a further 5 minutes, stirring frequently to prevent sticking. Add boiling water, cover and cook for 2 hours over very moderate heat. Add washed rice and olives and cook for another 15 to 20 minutes until liquid is absorbed. Stir in the parsley at last minute and serve hot.

MAKHBOUZ (Baked Veal)

Egypt

TO SERVE 4

1 lb. veal steak
2 onions, finely sliced
12 mushrooms (diced and sautéed in butter for 3 minutes)
1 bay leaf
1 teaspoon rock salt
1 gill double cream
8 oz. tomatoes, chopped and skinned
1 teaspoon chervil
5 tablespoons butter
1 teaspoon white pepper
1 leaf rosemary
6 oz. buttered white breadcrumbs

Cut veal into small cubes. Heat butter and brown meat for 5 minutes over medium heat.

Add tomatoes, seasoning, onion and herbs and simmer gently for 1 hour. Turn everything into a baking dish, add vegetables, top with buttered crumbs and bake — for 20 minutes. Finish off by browning crumbs under fierce grill.

MANTALI (Steak Mould)

Common to most Middle East countries

TO SERVE 4 — 6

1 1/2 lb. rump steak
2 oz. flour
2 large eggs, beaten
1 gill double cream
4 oz. French beans, diced
1/2 pint Sharp Sauce
salt and pepper
3 tablespoons olive oil
1/2 pint bone stock
1 tablespoon Worcester sauce
3 carrots, diced
8 oz. button mushrooms
1 lemon juice

Trim meat, remove any fat or skin. Wipe over with vinegar dampened cloth. Put through mincer 3 times.

Heat olive oil, add flour, stir well and cook on moderate heat for 5 minutes. Add stock and stir until thick. Add meat and eggs, seasoning and sauce. Cook for 5 minutes on reduced heat, then remove from fire.

Put through a wire sieve. Add cream and pour into a well oiled ring mould. Steam for 1 1/2 hours.

Cook carrots and beans in boiling salted water for 7 minutes, add vegetables and cook a further 5 minutes. Drain and toss in butter.

Turn out mould on a hot dish, coat with Sharp Sauce and fill centre with the vegetables. Serve with potatoes.

KOFTA BANDORA (Meatballs with Tomatoes)

Jordan

TO SERVE 4

1 lb. minced mutton
2 slices stale rye bread
1/4 pint light ale
3 tomatoes, skinned
1 tablespoon almond oil
flour for coating
1 large onion, minced
2 eggs
6 tablespoons butter

1 teaspoon garlic salt
1/2 teaspoon cayenne pepper
few springs parsley

Soak bread in very little ale for 5 minutes, then squeeze dry.

Put in a mixing bowl the meat, onion, bread, parsley, eggs, pepper and salt and knead all together for about 5 minutes. Oil palms of hands and shape mixture into large round balls, very slightly flattened. Flour both sides.

Heat butter, drop in balls and cook over low heat until nicely browned. Add chopped tomatoes and rest of ale and heat through. Transfer to oven and bake for 35 minutes at 350°F. — Regulo 4.

SAMBOUSICK

At least 12 hours before use, mix, set aside and let rise the following:
4 cups all-purpose flour
2 teaspoons baking power
4 teaspoons oil
2 teaspoons salt
2 eggs

Water enough to produce a soft dough.

Cook 1/2 kilo ground meat (lamb or beef) and a medium-size bunch of finely chopped parsley. After cooking, add 2 chopped, hard boiled eggs.

Roll dough 1/4 inch thick. In a straight line, spacing at four-inch intervals, place 1 teaspoon meat mixture. Fold dough over top of meat mixture, press around meat mixture. Using a pastry wheel, cut squares around the meat about 2 inches by 2 inches. Again, press edges tightly together.

Heat a low greased frying pan to very hot. Place one dough square at a time into the grease. Spoon grease over the top. The dough square will puff and when golden brown, turn until golden brown on both sides.

Remove from grease, drain and serve.

Prior to pastry wheels, Arab women would use the edge of pot lids to cut the dough squares. Even today some continue to make many small round pancakes of dough, filled with meat, rather than cutting squares. The same effect is achieved.

SAMBOUSA (Meat Pasties)

A dish from Mecca

TO SERVE 4 — 6

12 oz. plain flour
1 large onion
3 tablespoons water
1 large whole egg
3 pints bouillon (meat extract cubes may be used)
1 teaspoon paprika
1 egg yolk
1/2 pint yoghurt
4 oz. butter
8 oz. minced beef
2 teaspoons salt
1 teaspoon white pepper
caraway seeds for decoration

Sieve flour into mixing bowl. Make a well in centre, break whole egg into it and add egg yolk. Add salt and water. Knead to stiff dough, then leave aside for 2 hours.

Meanwhile, prepare filling for Manti by combining minced beef, finely chopped onions, salt and pepper.
When dough is ready, roll it out as thinly as

possible on a floured board. Cut into 2-inch squares, put a teaspoon of filling into each, fold over and seal with a little water. Brush with beaten egg, decorate with caraway seeds and cook in lightly oiled shallow dish in hot oven (400°F. — Regulo 6) until golden brown, about 20 minutes. Remove from oven and while hot, pour the bouillon over. Cover pan, put into slow oven (300°F. — Regulo 2) and cook until pastries are big and soft, and all stock soaked into them.

Empty yoghurt into mixing bowl and beat a few times with fork. Melt butter and add paprika. Sprinkle mixture over yoghurt and pour into individual glasses. Serve with hot Manti.

LAHMA BI AJEEN

TO SERVE 8 TO 10 PERSONS

Arab type of pizza with a meat filling. Delicious, dainty, elegant to serve at a party, these savories are also very easy to prepare with a simple bread dough.

DOUGH

1/2 oz. (1 cake) fresh yeast or
1 package dried yeast
1 cup lukewarm water
Pinch of sugar
3 1/2 cups all-purpose flour
1 teaspoon salt
2 1/2 tablespoons oil

Dissolve the yeast with a pinch of sugar in about 1/2 cup of the lukewarm water specified above. Leave aside in a warm place for about 10 minutes, or until the mixture begins to bubble.

In the meantime, sift the flour and salt into a large warmed mixing bowl. Make a well in the centre and add the oil and the yeast mixture. Work the dough vigorously, adding the remaining lukewarm water gradually to make a soft dough. Knead vigorously for about 15 minutes until the dough is pliable and elastic, and comes away from the side of the bowl. Cover with a damp cloth and set aside in a warm, draft-free place for 2 to 3 hours, or until doubled in bulk. To prevent a dry crust from forming on the surface, put a little oil in the bottom of the bowl and roll the ball of dough in it to coat the entire surface before leaving it to rest.

While waiting for the dough to rise, prepare the filling:

1 lb. onions, finely chopped
Oil
1 1/2 lbs. lean lamb or beef, ground
1 lb. fresh tomatoes, skinned and chopped, or a 1-lb. can whole tomatoes
3 tablespoons tomato paste
1 teaspoon sugar
3/4 teaspoon ground allspice
1-2 tablespoons lemon juice
Salt and black pepper
4 tablespoons finely chopped parsley (optional)
Pinch of cayenne pepper (optional)

filling made on its own tastes
Very nice with rice & Chickpea
Puree from "Middle Eastern" cookbook
p 279

MARGOOG A DELICIOUS SAUDI DISH

Arabs use Qamh flour for their bread and pastry. Qamh is the Arabic equivalent of flour. While visibly similar (and necessary for certain Arabic recipes which as Ataif), of course it is not satisfactory for western pastries.

Qamh in its original form is a small tan, perfectly formed oblong seed commonly known as a whole wheat kernel. When ground, Qamh may be coarse or fine in flour form.

In its coarse state ground Qamh is called jareesh and the finer grind is called burghul, which is a fairly common western grain. Though jareesch is larger than burghul, both are irregular in shape, slightly shiny and yellow of white in colouring and both are used as additions to soups, stews and vegetables or cooked alone similar to rice. In addition, burghul is used in the popular Arabic salad, Tabbouleh.

To start you off in this purely Saudi dish hailing from the Najd region, the dish is considered a delicacy because of the lengthy time necessary for preparation. Favoured in cold weather, you will notice the recipe obtained direct from a Saudi kitchen.

MARGOOG

10 servings
2 cups Qamh
water
salt to taste
1/2 kilo meat, lamb or beef in large chunks (bones are alright)

oil
3 medium onions, chopped
3 medium tomatoes, chopped
2 small cans tomato paste
1 cube chicken broth
3 cloves garlic
1 tsp. coriander
1 tsp. Kumon
1 tsp. cinnamon
2 hot peppers, fresh red or green, whole
5 small squash, fresh and whole
10 string beans, fresh and whole

In a large bowl mix Qamh and water to a heavy dough consistency, adding salt to taste. Knead five minutes, set aside to rise for one hour.

In a large pot brown onion and meat in oil. Add tomatoes, tomato paste, chicken broth, seasonings and hot peppers. Mix well. Add 4 cups water and simmer for one hour.

DAWOUD BASHA

Lebanon

2 2/3 lbs. lean lamb (taken from the leg)
2 1/5 lbs. small onions, peeled and left whole
10 oz. butter
2 1/2 tbs. salt
3 tbs. flour
4 oz. lemon juice
1/2 tsp. spices
1 1/5 pts. boiling water
2 oz. pine nuts

Grind meat as fine as possible, putting it through the grinder at least three times. Add a little of the salt, then form the meat in the shape of large marbles. Heat butter in a skillet and fry meat, and when brown, remove to a pot. Fry onions in the same butter till it is a golden brown and add to the pot. Drain out the butter left in the skillet leaving enough to brown the flour. Add water to the flour and let come to a hard boil, then pour it over the meat and onions. Add rest of salt and spices. Cook over moderate heat till meat is done about 2 minutes before removing it, cover and cook over moderate heat for 10 minutes. Remove from heat, add the meat, seasoning, herbs and marrow pulp and cook for 7 minutes. Remove from heat.

Drain and wipe marrows and stiff tightly with the meat mixture and arrange side by side in a wide bottom saucepan. Add rest of fat, 1 gill of stock, cover closely and cook for 15 minutes over moderate heat. Add tomatoes and remaining stock, cover and cook a further hour. Serve hot in own liquor garnished with whole leaves of dill.

2 oz. salt
1 lb. butter plus a piece of mutton
2 oz. flour for the sauce
2/3 pt. water for the sauce
1/2 tsp. white pepper

Rub lamb with salt and pepper inside out and truss and tie legs or have it in a kneeling position in the baking pan. Pour the melted butter over it and place pieces of the fat on top. Place it in an oven and bake it. Prepare the sauce.

In the meantime, after the Qamh has risen, lightly coat your fingers with oil and roll the dough into smooth, dime-sized balls. Flatten each separately on a large tray.

After the meat sauce has simmered for one hour, add squash, string beans and each pancake individually to the sauce. Continue to simmer for about another 45 minutes, adding water if necessary. Salt and pepper to taste.

CASSEROLE OF COD FILLETS

Egypt

TO SERVE 6

1 1/2 cod fillets
8 oz. white breadcrumbs
1 teaspoon celery salt
1 teaspoon cayenne pepper
1/2 pint single cream
4 oz. soft butter
1 teaspoon paprika pepper
6 tomatoes, halved and skinned

Arrange the cleaned and wiped fillets in a baking dish and pour over them half the cream.

Mix together the bread crumbs, butter, salt and cayenne pepper and spread across the fillets. Pour over the rest of the cream and sprinkle with paprika. Garnish with the tomato halves. Bake at 375°F. — Regulo 4, for 40 minutes. Serve hot.

SATED LAMB LIVER

Arabian Gulf

TO SERVE 4

400g (14 oz.) lamb liver
dash of ginger juice
1 tablespoon cooking wine
4 tablespoons cornstarch
1 onion (cut into 8 pieces)
1 clove garlic (sliced)
3 tablespoons oil (food oil)
1/2 teaspoons sugar
1/4 teaspoon salt
2 1/2 tablespoons hot sauce (ready bottled)

Cooking time 30 minutes

Soak liver in water. Drain well. Cut into bite size slices. Season with wine. Mix in starch. Fry in oil. Put it aside. Heat new oil. Fry onion and garlic. Add liver. Add the hot sauce of your choice with the sugar and salt. Mix and turn off heat.

KABLAMA

Lebanon

TO SERVE 4

1 lb. calves' liver
2 oz. butter
8 button onions
2 teaspoons flour
salt and pepper
1/4 pint (U.S. 2/3 cup) boiling water
lemon juice
2 cloves garlic
chopped mint
cinnamon

Cut the liver in slices and toss it in butter. Put it into a flameproof dish. Toss the onions in the same butter till they are golden all round. Add a little flour and stir it in. Pour this over the liver. Add the salt and pepper and the boiling water and cook over a fierce flame — not too long, or you will make the liver tough. Add a squeeze of lemon juice, the garlic finely chopped and a little mint (less if it is dried than if it is fresh). Before serving sprinkle on a pinch of cinnamon.

LSANAT (Lambs Tongues with Cream)

Lebanon

TO SERVE 4

3 shallots, chopped
1 gill milk
1/4 pint single cream
1 tablespoon dry white wine
bouquet garni (1/2 teaspoon thyme, bay leaf)
2 tablespoons butter
2 tablespoons flour
1 tablespoon tomato puree
1 lb. lambs tongues (stud with slivers of garlic)

Heat lambs' tongues and arrange on a serving dish. Cover with the sauce and glaze under a hot grill for 5 to 7 minutes. Serve hot

SAWANI (Casserole of Lamb Shanks)

Common to most Middle East countries

TO SERVE 6

2 lb. lamb shanks
4 oz. sliced mushrooms
4 tablespoons good fat
3 sliced onions
1 teaspoon cayenne pepper
1 pint bone stock
1 gill dry red wine
6 young carrots
celery salt to taste

Heat fat in deep saucepan and brown lamb shanks. Season and add stock. Cover closely and simmer over gentle heat for 1 1/4 hours.

Add vegetables, cover and cook on moderate heat for a further hour. Serve hot in own juices.

TAS KEBAB (Lamb Stew)

Common to all Middle East countries

TO SERVE 6

3 lb. top-part leg lamb
1 pint bone stock
3 tomatoes, chopped and skinned
2 cloves crushed garlic
3 onions, chopped
3 tablespoons butter
1 level teaspoon fresh thyme, minced
salt and pepper

Cut meat, free of fat, into small cubes. Sprinkle with seasoning and thyme and leave in a cool place for 5 hours.

Melt butter and fry onions for 5 minutes. Add meat, cover pan tightly, and cook over very low heat for 25 minutes, shaking pan occasionally to prevent sticking.

Cut tomatoes small and add with the garlic to meat mixture. Season and add half the stock. Cook for 2 1/2 hours over very low heat, and until meat is tender, and add the remaining stock after the first hour of cooking.

For last 15 minutes of cooking time, uncover, increase heat and boil rapidly until liquid is reduced to a few tablespoons. This will take only a few minutes.

KAWAREH BI HUMMUS
(Calf's Feet and Chickpeas)

This dish is loved all over the Middle East. The dish is sometimes served as a soup, prepared with only 1 calf's foot, and more water.

2 calf's feet
4 tablespoons oil
Salt and black pepper
1 teaspoon turmeric
1 1/2 cups chick-peas, soaked overnight
2 hard-boiled eggs, sliced

Wash and scrape the feet thoroughly. Blanch them in boiling water until a scum has formed. Throw out the water. Heat the oil in a large saucepan and fry the feet in it for a few minutes until colored all over. Add salt and pepper to taste, turmeric, and the soaked and drained chick-peas. Cover with water, bring to the boil, and simmer gently until the meat is practically falling off the bones, for about 4 hours. The time can be reduced about 3/4 hour with a pressure cooker. Bone the feet if you wish and return the meat to the pan.

Serve with a light salad and, if you like, garnished with hard-boiled eggs.

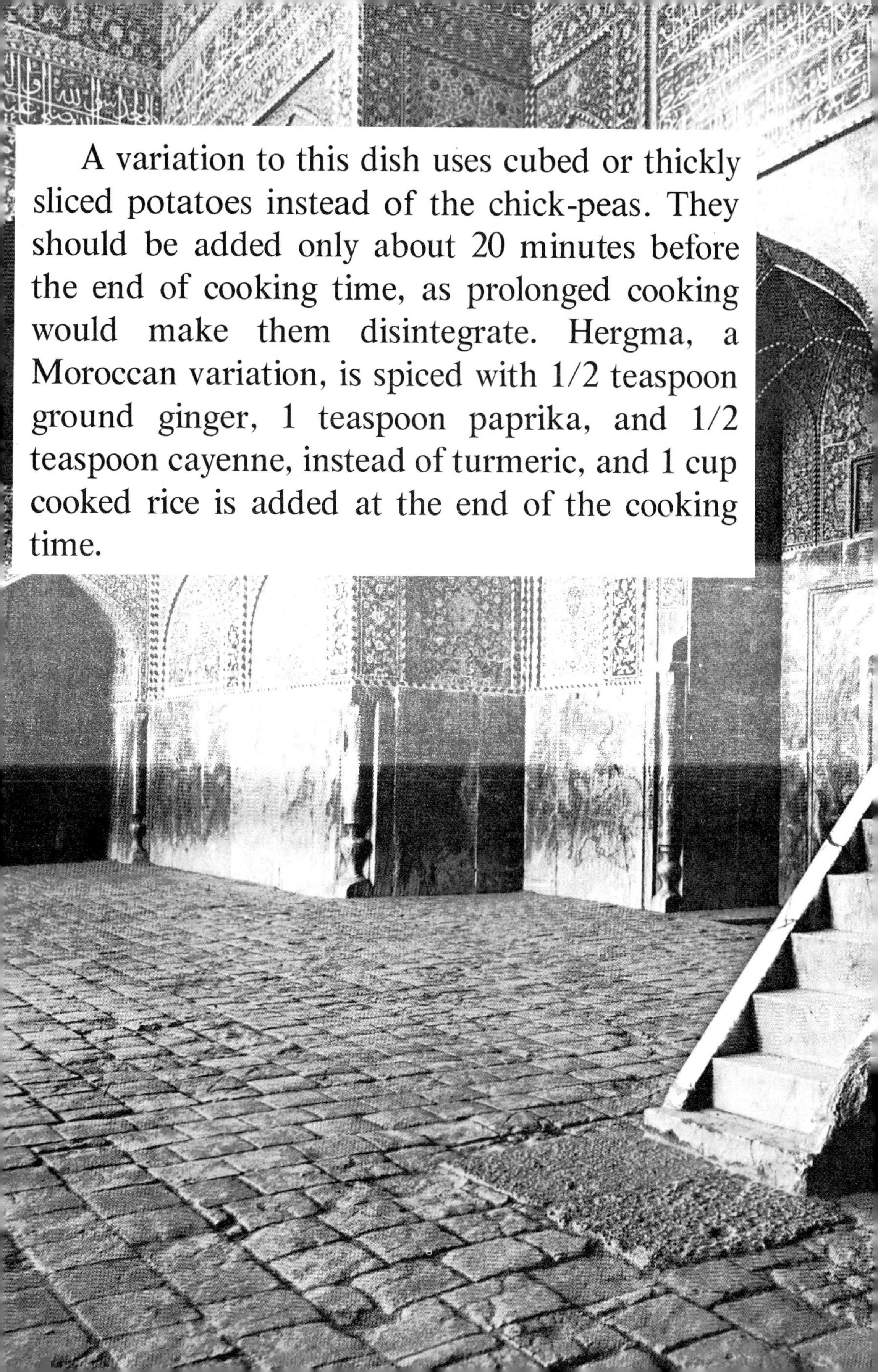

A variation to this dish uses cubed or thickly sliced potatoes instead of the chick-peas. They should be added only about 20 minutes before the end of cooking time, as prolonged cooking would make them disintegrate. Hergma, a Moroccan variation, is spiced with 1/2 teaspoon ground ginger, 1 teaspoon paprika, and 1/2 teaspoon cayenne, instead of turmeric, and 1 cup cooked rice is added at the end of the cooking time.

SHASHLIK

Common to all Middle East countries

TO SERVE 6

2 lb. top part leg lamb
24 button mushrooms
6 spring onions
skewers
1/2 pint olive oil
4 onions, finely chopped
salt and paprika pepper

Clean meat from bone, remove skin and fat and cut into 1 inch cubes. Cut trimmed meat into fairly large pieces and fry in butter until both sides are pink. Remove from heat and leave aside.

Add onions, carrots, seasoning and half the dill and cook over low heat for 25 minutes, turning meat from time to time. Add wine and tomatoes and cover with grease-proof paper. Put on lid and simmer gently for 1 hour. Remove meat and keep hot.

Sauté potatoes for 5 minutes in clarified fat and add, with thyme and peas, to the liquor left in saucepan.

Now take some grease-proof paper (cut to more than double the size of each piece of meat) and lay a piece of meat in the centre. Cover with enough vegetables, pour over a little liquor from saucepan, twist ends of paper so that everything is well sealed and none of the liquid can escape, and arrange side by side on a baking tray. Sprinkle with a little hot water and bake for 15 minutes in a very hot oven (450°F. — Regulo 8).

Remove from papers and serve with a sprinkling of dill.

Marinate meat cubes in olive oil, salt, onions and paprika for 24 hours. Allow 6 cubes meat to each skewer, and keep them 1/4 inch apart. Grill for 6 minutes turning skewer all the time.

Sauté mushrooms in the seasoned olive oil and serve as a garnishing. Cut spring onions small and scatter over.

TAFTA KOFTA (Beef balls in the Pan)

Common to all Middle East countries

TO SERVE 4

3 slices stale bread
2 cloves crushed garlic
3 tablespoons grated cheese
salt and pepper
chicken fat for frying
1 lb. beef
2 onions, grated
1 teaspoon cayenne pepper
2 eggs
1 tablespoon dill, chopped
1 gill grape juice

Soak bread in grape juice and squeeze dry in hands.

Put meat 3 times through mincer, add bread and put through mincer again. Add all other ingredients, except chicken fat, and knead for 10 minutes. Wet palms of hands with leftover grape juice and shape mixture into small balls.

Heat fat to boiling point and put in balls. Reduce heat to low and cook until both sides are well browned, about 30 minutes for whole operation.

NECK OF LAMB STUFFED AND BOILED

Saudi Arabia

2 1/5 lbs. meat from the neck
3 1/5 oz. rice
1/2 lb. meat, fatty and cut fine
2 tbs. salt
1/2 tsp. pepper, sweet and hot
1/2 tsp. saffron
4 oz. snobar (optional)
1 tbs. rosewater
3 1/5 pts. water
1 oz. water for stuffing

Open the neck so that it will be in the shape of a sack, the two layers not separated. Stuff it with rice, meat, snobar, salt, pepper and rose water (mixing all those ingredients well first). Sew up the opening and place in a pot and cover with water. Cook over high heat and skim it well as the skim appears. Keep on high few minutes longer, then reduce heat to medium and cook until done. Slice it before serving into round slices with the stuffing in the centre. Serve hot. The broth becomes a delicious soup by adding a little rice to it.

SHEEP'S HEAD

This is a popular Middle Eastern dish which, I have been told, was quite well known in England and Scotland in the past, particularly during the last war when meat was scarce.

Ask the butcher to remove the part around the sheep's nose altogether, as this is extremely hard to clean. Clean the sheep's head carefully, singeing off any hair and scraping with a sharp knife.

One way of preparing it after this is to split it in half lengthwise and remove the brains. (These can be cleaned and cooked separately). Blanch the head in boiling water until a scum has formed on the surface, and drain. Rub with a little rose water or lemon juice.

Put the two halves in a pot with an onion, water to cover, and salt and pepper to taste. Bring to the boil and simmer until the meat is very tender, about 3 hours; or cook in a pressure cooker for about 1 hour. Serve as it is, or bone it and serve the meat separately.

Another, rather tastier way is to clean the head as above and roast it whole in the oven. Rub it with salt and pepper, and brush with melted butter. Roast until well done in a moderately hot oven (400°F), turning it occasionally and basting generously with more melted butter. It will take from 1 to 2 hours, depending on the age of the animal.

Serve the head whole on a platter, or if you wish, remove the meat and serve it garnished with paprika.

Serve with salads.

THE MOST DELICIOUS SAUDI ARABIAN DISH **SALEEG:**

Saleeg is one of the most famous meals among the Arabs and Bedouins of the Desert of Saudi Arabia. It is said to be refreshing and a food of vitality; besides, it can be easily digested.

Quantities:

A meal for five persons

RICE	5 cups (one cup per person)
MILK	10 cups (2 cups of milk per cup of rice)
SALT	8 teaspoons
BUTTER	4 tablespoons

A SMALL SHEEP OR HALF A SHEEP

Clean and sprinkle inside of sheep with salt and pepper. Put plenty of butter in a big pan. Brown the sheep on all sides. Empty the pan from the remaining butter. Put enough milk in the pan to cover half the sheep. Cover and cook for 4-6 hours until meat is well done. Turn the sheep occasionally while cooking.

After the sheep, or the half sheep, is very well done remove it from the pan.

Measure 10 cups from the boiling milk. Put them in an ordinary pan.

Add 8 teaspoons of salt (or as much as you like)

Add 4 tablespoons of butter

Add 1 teaspoon of pepper
Add 1 teaspoon of cardamon

Cover the pan and put it back on fire to boil for 20 minutes.

Pour all the rice in a big silver tray and place the well done sheep on top of it.

LET EVERYBODY SERVE HIMSELF.

THE FAMOUS SHAWIRMAH

Damascus

Take about 44 lbs. of veal, cut from the leg of a young beef which was butchered 2 days earlier.

Slice meat into round, thin slices about 7 inches in diameter and about 1 inch thick. Cut pieces of fat the same size and thickness as the lean meat.

Marinate the meat in mixture of the following ingredients:

1 tbs. cardamom seed
1 tbs. mastic
1 1/2 tbs. cinnamon
1 tbs. nutmeg
1 tbs. white pepper
1/2 tbs. black pepper
1 lb. red onions
5 bay leaves
2 oz. garlic
1 qt. lemon
1 pt. olive oil
2 pts. vinegar, good quality
1 tbs. cloves
1 1/2 lbs. salt

Soak cardamom seed for 6 hours, then grind it fine with its skin. Add 1 tbs. salt to the mastic and pound together until very fine. Chop fine.

Take part of the spices, salt and pepper and rub into the meat and fat. Place meat in a glass or earthenware container and marinate in a mixture of the above ingredients with onions. Soak for 24 hours keeping it in a refrigerator the temperature of which is 5 degrees centigrade above zero. Stir the meat from time to time.

At the end of 24 hours, take out of refrigerator and keep at room temperature for 2 hours. All ingredients must warm up to room temperature.

Stick the meat on long skewers or place on a revolving rotisserie. If using skewers, they must be the kind that turns automatically and constantly while the meat is broiling. In sticking the meat on skewers, put one piece of fat between four pieces of lean meat. The skewer must be perpendicular to the fire and very near to it. This could be a hot charcoal fire or strong electric or gas fire. Place it so that the meat is facing the fire.

KIBBEH NAYYA
(Raw Minced Lamb with crushed wheat)

Lebanon — Syria — Jordan

TO SERVE 6

10 oz. fine BURGHUL (crushed wheat)
1 lb. lean boneless lamb, preferably leg of lamb, finely minced 3 times
teaspoon ground allspice
A pinch of ground nutmeg, preferably freshly grated nutmeg
A pinch of cayenne pepper
1 teaspoon salt
Freshly ground black pepper

GARNISH

pint olive oil
2 small onions, peeled and cut into quarters

Place the BURGHUL in a bowl or pan, pour in enough cold water to cover it completely and let it soak for about 10 minutes. Then drain it in a sieve or colander lined with a double thickness of dampened cheesecloth. Wrap the BURGHUL in the cheesecloth and squeeze it dry. Drop the BURGHUL into a deep mixing bowl, add the lamb and, moistening your hands from time to time with cold water, knead until the mixture is smooth. Knead in the allspice, nutmeg, cayenne, salt and a few grindings of pepper and taste for seasoning. Divide the mixture into 8 equal portions and, moistening your hands with cold water, shape them into round flat cakes about 4 inches in diameter and 1/2 inch thick. Place the cakes on individual serving plates and make a well in the centre of each cake with your thumbs. Pour 1 1/2 tablespoons of oil into each opening and let it flow over the surface of the meat. Garnish the KIBBEH NAYYA with quarter onions and serve at once.

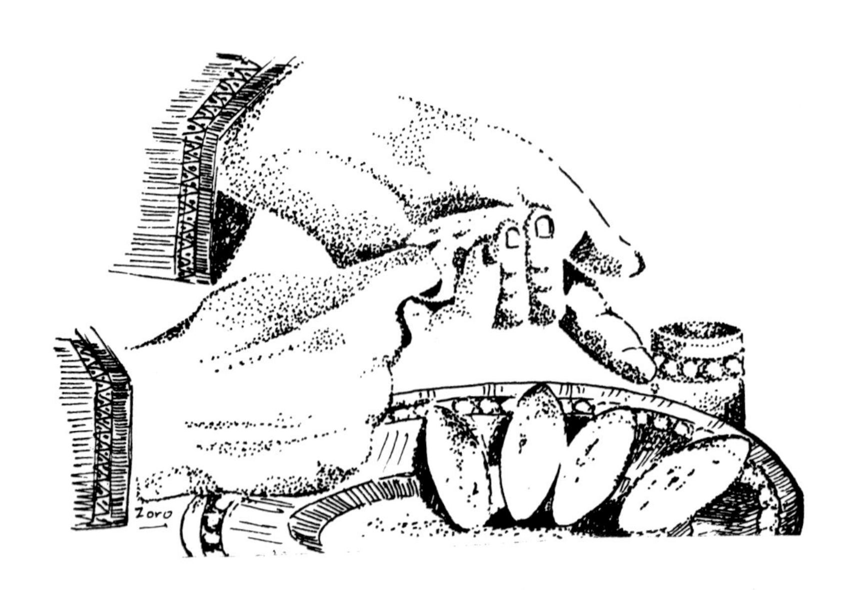

KOFTA MESHWEYA
(Grilled Ground Meat on Skewers)

Each country and each area in the Middle East has its favorite flavorings for kofta. *Here is a basic recipe, giving a few simple alternative seasonings.*

2 lbs. beef, lamb, or a mixture of both, ground
2 onions, grated
1-2 eggs
Salt and black pepper
Optional seasonings: 1 teaspoon
ground cinnamon, or 1
teaspoon ground allspice, or 1/2
teaspoon ground cumin and 1/2
teaspoon ground coriander

Put the meat through the grinder two or three times, then mix together with the remaining ingredients in a bowl, and pound or knead until very, very smooth. The art of making this delicious meat dish lies in achieving an extremely soft and pasty texture.

Take smallish lumps of the mixture and pat them into sausage shapes around skewers (preferably the flat-edged sword type). If grilling over a barbecue, wait until the charcoal has stopped smoking and glows dull red before you place the skewers over it. Try not to let the meat touch the metal, and make sure the grill is well oiled to prevent the meat from sticking to it. Turn the skewers until the *kofta* are cooked and browned all over.

Serve nestling in warm Arab bread or pitta to catch the juices, or with plain rice, and accompanied by salad.

Grill rows of shish kebab (above) and kofta together. Serve them on a bed of parsley or chervil, sprinkled with finely chopped onions. This is often served in cafes as *kofta wa kebab.*

When you count the gifts of God, you never finish calculating.

Very nice + tasty.
(not too sweet.)

BEEF WITH NUTS AND RAISINS

Egypt

1 pound beef, ground
1 teaspoon monosodium glutamate
1 teaspoon salt
1 tablespoon curry powder
1 cup onion slices
1/2 cup diced green pepper
2 tablespoons butter
1 cup seedless raisins
2/3 cup cashew nuts
2 bay leaves
1 can (1 pound) peas
1 can (4 ounces)
pimiento, coarsely cut
1 orange, sliced
hot cooked rice
chutney

SPRINKLE beef with monosodium glutamate, salt, and curry powder

COOK onion and green pepper in butter until tender

ADD beef. Cook, stirring, until browned

ADD raisins, nuts, and bay leaves

DRAIN peas. Add liquid to beef mixture. (Reserve peas)

SIMMER for 20 minutes
ADD peas and pimiento. Place orange slices on top
SIMMER for 10 minutes
SERVE with hot cooked rice and chutney
YIELD 3 servings

ROAST LAMB

Saudi Arabia

1 small lamb about 17-18 lbs.,
killed and prepared a day in advance

Melt butter designated for the stuffing in a skillet and fry onions, chopped meat, and nuts. When it is fried remove to a pot and add salt, saffron, rice and water. Boil about 5 minutes over high heat, then reduce heat to moderate and cook until done.

Salt the lamb inside out and rub in with pepper. Stuff with the above stuffing and sew and truss or have it kneeling on its foreleg in a baking pan. Pour melted butter over it and put in moderately hot oven and bake until done. Baste it often with melted butter and some of its own juice. Cover all the top part of it with foil. Turn lamb from time to time.

When lamb is done remove baking pan and keep hot in another container. Drain out all but a very little of the butter and sauce in the pan in which the lamb was baked. Place pan on top of stove and add flour and stir until it turns brown. Pour over it the liquid that was drained out and saved and let it boil till it begins to thicken. Pour it into a strainer. Return the strained sauce to boil a little longer over low heat and keep hot until ready to serve. If much butter appears on top of sauce, skim it off the top. Serve lamb on large tray or platter and sauce in a separate container.

ROAST TONGUE OF VEAL

Lebanon

2 medium tongues of veal or
5 sheep tongues
3 tbs. rock salt
1 1/2 tbs. salt
7 1/2 oz. butter
2 tbs. flour
8 oz. boiling water
12 oz. carrot water
12 oz. carrots, leek and onions
1 lb. ripe tomatoes

Wash tongues well and rub them with rock salt, leave them in an earthenware container for 24 hours. Then take them out, wash them again and put them in a pot to boil. After removing the skim add tomatoes and the rest of the vegetables and cook together with the tongues till all are cooked. Take tongues out and remove their skin and cut them to pieces.

Melt butter in a pan and brown the tongues in it. Remove tongues, drain out some of the butter, then add flour. When it browns a little add boiling water. Cook till sauce thickens, then run it through a fine strainer and return the strained sauce to boil some more and keep it hot on very low heat till it is time to serve. You can serve the tongues with sauce over them or serve the sauce separately. You may also arrange pieces of tongue on a platter with puree potatoes or vegetables on the same platter.

Say: O my Lod; let my entry be the Gate of Truth, and let my exit be by the Gate of Truth, and grant me from Thy Presence, a helping power.
And Say: Truth has come and falsehood perished: for untruth is bound to perish.
(Quran 17, 80 — 81).

243 *Saudi cooks preparing the famous Mihammar in a ground oven.*

MIHAMMAR (Small Lamb)

Saudi Arabia

2 lbs. lean meat pounded or ground very fine
2 lbs. rice (Uncle Bens)
4 cups of water
1 teaspoon pepper
2 tablespoons salt
5 boiled eggs (do not cut them)
5 tablespoons of butter
1 cup of raisins (sweet and small)

This meal comes second to the SALEEG in popularity among the people of Saudi Arabia.

Buy a small lamb or half a lamb at your butcher shop. Clean it and sprinkle the inside with salt and pepper.

Mix the ground meat with salt, pepper, egg whites, butter, peanuts. This mixture must be mixed by hand very well.

Stuff the lamb with this mixture and sew it. Melt butter. Place the lamb in a suitable baking pan and pour the melted butter over, then insert it into a hot oven to brown on all sides. Cover pan and reduce heat to low and let cook.

Add three cups of water.

Then expose the other side and baste with yoghurt until the yoghurt is dry, for 6 hours.

NADI (Lamb with Spices)

Dish from Medina

TO SERVE 4

1 lb. minced lamb
2 tablespoons butter
2 teaspoons ground allspice
1 lemon juice
peel of orange, cut small
3 tablespoons walnuts, finely chopped
salt and pepper

Heat butter and brown minced lamb for 10 minutes on medium heat. Add orange juice and cook a further 5 minutes. Add peel, walnuts and seasoning, stir well, cover and cook over a very low heat for 25 minutes.

Pile in centre of hot dish, surround with a ring of plain rice and dust with allspice.

Chop shallots finely and cook in butter until soft. Add flour and stir well. Add gradually the milk and cream, allow to thicken and stir frequently to avoid lumpiness. Remove from heat and stir in the wine and the tomato puree. Add seasoning and herbs. Return to heat and simmer over hot water for 35 minutes until mixture is a nice creamy consistency.

Have a sharp knife, ready and cut the edges of

the meat as it broils. Serve it unwrapped in loaves of Arab bread on plates. Sprinkle over it some of its drippings which has gathered in the tray in which the revolving skewer is anchored.

A Saudi cook cooking rice of Nadi in a ground oven.

An outdoor party in Saudi Arabia.

THE ART OF RICE COOKING IN THE ARAB KITCHEN

Few other foods are as easy to assimilate and to digest. Contrary to general opinion the white milled grain of rice is not 'all starch, anyway'; it contains a high proportion of vegetable proteins. With today's milling of rice the starch content is in many cases reduced and then no washing is necessary. The milling is a cleaning process. Also, rice cooked in an open pan tends to lose food value if excess water is drained off after cooking. So, it is best to cook rice in the smallest amount of water: this ensures its best flavour and guards the nutrient within the grain.

Plain boiled rice.

With so many different kinds of rice it is impossible to give one way of cooking that covers them all. The brown, unpolished rice, for instance, takes longer than any of the white varieties. If you use the quickcook variety, follow the directions on the packet, and do not leave it a minute longer on the stove, for these preprepared grains really do cook quickly, and easily become a soggy mess. However, if you follow a few basic rules, there is no reason why you should not cook rice perfectly: rice that is fluffy and dry, without lumps or the grains clogging together.

1. The type of rice: for curries buy the best type of long grain rice available.
2. The vessel used for cooking: use a saucepan or casserole of heavy meal, and until you reach the stage where you can cook rice under any conditions, or in any pan, keep to the same pan and get to know its reaction to rice, water, heat and stirring.
3. Amount of water: measure this carefully according to the cooking method you adopt, and until you learn to judge it by sight.
4. The degree of heat for cooking: except for the short time at the beginning needed to boil the water, the heat used is always gentle.
5. Stirring: the only time you stir is when you first put the rice grains into the boiling water. Resist the impulse to stir in the final stages of cooking, for this can damage the grains and spoil the dry, fluffy appearance expected as an end result.

Here are some well-tried methods of cooking plain boiled rice. There is certain to be one of these, at least, that suits you. A couple of attempts with it should give you any confidence you need, and then it is worthwhile adopting it for future use.

Notes

When working out the quantity of rice required, remember that in cooking it expands to three times its weight.

For extra whiteness add lemon juice to the cooking water.

When you stir rice, and this is only in the early stages of cooking, use a fork and not a spoon. Do not take off the lid until the end of the prescribed cooking time to look at it.

Where necessary, rinse the cooked rice with hot water to separate grains and spread on a flat tray or large dish and place in a warm oven to keep hot. Processed or converted rice, which absorbs all the water, does not need rinsing.

rice of colours in the Arab world rice cooking.

Boiled rice:
little water
method 1

AMERICAN
2 1/2 cups rice
5 1/2 cups water
1 teaspoon salt
Cooking time: 18-20 minutes
Serves: 4-6

Add the rice to the rapidly boiling water to which salt has been added; stir with a fork until is boiling again. Cover saucepan, keep boiling for about 1 minute. Lower the heat to its lowest, and cook until done. This should be in about 16-18 minutes. Test a grain with fingers or teeth. If underdone, sprinkle a tablespoon of water on it, and leave to cook for 2 minutes more. When rice is tender, take it off heat, but keep covered. Let it stand for 5-10 minutes, then serve. This should give it time to absorb all the water.

Boiled rice:
little water
method 2

AMERICAN
4 1/2 cups water
1 teaspoon salt
2 1/2 cups rice.
Cooking time: 15 minutes
Serves: 4-6

Bring the water with salt to the boil, add rice, stir. When boiling again, cover well. A damp cloth, covering the pot under the lid, will ensure that no steam escapes. Simmer on a low heat. After 14 minutes remove to a cool place and let stand for 10 minutes. Then serve.

Boiled rice:
more water
method 1

AMERICAN
10 cups water
1 teaspoon salt
2 1/2 cups rice
Cooking time: 18-20 minutes
Serves: 4-6

Bring water with salt to the boil. Add rice. Leave to boil until rice is done — about 18 minutes, but test. If tender, add 1/2 pint (3 dl) cold water immediately, and strain the rice. Put in a warm covered dish and serve after one minute.

Boiled rice:
more water
method 2

AMERICAN
2 1/2 cups rice
10 cups water, salt added to taste
Cooking time: 15 minutes
Serves: 4-6

Dribble the rice through the fingers slowly into a pan of fast-boiling water. Boil at a gallop, 10 minutes, or until the grains are just tender. Pour in a cup of cold water to stop the boiling. Drain rice through a sieve and put in a dry pan. Cover with a linen cloth and let it stand on a very low heat or in the oven with the door open until the rice is quite dry. Shake the pan occasionally. This method breaks the slowboiling rule, but there are people who swear by it.

To reheat leftover boiled rice.

If you have a small quantity of rice left over and wish to combine it with freshly cooked rice, add the leftover rice to the rice you are boiling 3 minutes before you remove it from the stove.

If you have a large quantity of rice to reheat, bring plenty of water to the boil, and keep boiling. Add the leftover rice to the water, stir once with a fork, and leave for 5-10 seconds. Drain; keep covered in a hot dish for 1/2 minute before serving.

RICE WITH LAMB

Syria

5	cups boiling water
2	cups raw rice

1 teaspoon salt
1/2 cup nut meats
1/4 cup butter
1 1/2 pounds lamb, cubed
2 tablespoons minced mint
1/2 teaspoon cinnamon

POUR 2 cups boiling water over rice. Add salt. Cover. Let stand for 4 hours.

SAUTÉ nut meats in butter in deep saucepan for 5 minutes. Remove nuts. Reserve.

BROWN lamb in same pan. Remove lamb. Reserve.

ADD remaining 3 cups boiling water to butter remaining in pan. Bring to boil. Add rice and water in which it was soaked

BOIL 5 minutes. Reduce heat and simmer until water is absorbed and rice tender

PLACE nuts and lamb on top of rice. Sprinkle with mint. Cover.

REHEAT

SPRINKLE with cinnamon before serving. Toss to mix

YIELD 6 servings.

RICE WITH LAMB (Roz Walahm)

Kuwait

Ingredients:

3 lbs. 4 oz. meat of young lamb with its bones
1 1/10 lbs. rice
6 oz. butter
3 1/2 tsp. salt
1 tsp. pepper
2 pts. boiling water
(6 1/2 pts. for American rice)

Cut meat into pieces so that each piece might weigh around 2 1/2 oz. Fry in hot butter. Add salt and pepper and boiling water. Boil over moderate heat until meat is tender. Add rice and continue to cook over low heat until done. With very little stirring, turn contents onto a platter. Serve hot with laban.

MEATS & RICE

RICE WITH MILK

Saudi Arabia

TO SERVE 4

7 pts. milk
7 oz. rice
2 oz. rose water
1/2 pt. cold water
1 1/10 lbs. sugar

Strain milk into a pot and bring to a boil. Add rice and water and let it cook over low heat about 50 minutes. Increase heat and stir until it thickens and rice is done. Add sugar and at last the rose water and boil a little longer. Pour into wide platters or individual dessert plates and cool. Fruits canned in syrup like pears and apricots are served with this dessert.

Note: The above dish may be prepared without sugar and when serving, offer confectioner's sugar with it.

Rice with milk may be baked. Prepare it the same may as above but add 1 oz. starch to the rice and milk. Pour into Pyrex or earthenware dishes and put in hot oven till the top of dessert is a reddish brown.

RICE WITH RUMP OR SHIN OF LAMB AND GOURDS

Lebanon

10 oz. rice
2 1/5 lbs. rump or shin of lamb with bones (meat must be free of fat)
2 pts. 12 oz. water (to boil the meat)
10 oz. gourds cut into pieces or whole if it is small size
3 tsp. salt.

Boil meat with bones in water to which salt has been added. Skim. Add gourds, and let cook until meat is done. Remove bones. After removing bones add rice which has been soaked. Stir lightly and allow to boil hard first then remove to moderate heat until it is cooked. Serve hot.

Note: The amount of broth must not exceed a pint but should be slightly under a pint. If you have more broth than that, continue boiling till it is reduced to under a pint.

RICE AND SPINACH IN BUTTER OR OIL

Common to all Middle East countries

4 lbs. 6 oz. spinach
1 1/4 lbs. rice, washed and soaked
9 oz. finely chopped onions
3 tsp. salt
7 oz. butter or 10 oz. oil
1/4 tsp. sweet and hot pepper
1 pt. 15 oz. boiling water
(6pts boiling water if American rice is used)

Allow oil, or butter, to become very hot in a pot large enough to hold the spinach. When onions begin to brown, add spinach which had been washed well and cut fine. Stir regularly with a wire spoon for about 10 minutes then move it to moderate heat and add salt and pepper. Stir occasionally. When spinach is about cooked, add rice and boiling water. Cook over moderate heat until rice is done.

Note: If prepared in oil, serve cold. Otherwise serve hot.

RICE WITH RUMP OF LAMB BUTTER

Lebanon

2 lbs. shin of lamb with bones
6 oz. butter
1 1/4 lbs. rice
2 pts. boiling water
3 tsp. salt

Cut meat in such a way that each shin remains whole. Put butter in a copper pot; add meat and bones and brown over high heat. Turn meat so that all sides are brown. Add salt and water and let it boil hard over high heat. Reduce the heat to moderate and let meat cook till it is done. Now take out bones and add rice which has been soaked. Cook until rice is done. Leave near heat till it is time to serve it.

Note: Yoghurt may be served with this dish.

LAHEM MUQADDAD (Lamb on a Skewer)

Common to all Middle East countries

TO SERVE 4

1 lb. lamb, minced
1/2 teaspoon thyme
1/2 teaspoon white pepper
1 large onion juice
2 eggs
1 teaspoon garlic salt
2 tablespoons olive oil
2 tablespoons chives, chopped

Grease skewer by running through a piece of suet.

Mix all ingredients well together, with exception of olive oil and chives, and knead for a few minutes.

Grease palms of hands with olive oil and shape mixture into sausages. Brush well with oil, thread carefully on skewer and grill for 6 minutes, turning all the time.

Serve garnished with the chives.

A view in a Saudi Arabian oasis.

LAHEM TALI LAMB (Dish from Taif)

Saudi Arabia

TO SERVE 6

6 lamb cutlets
1/2 teaspoon chives
1 oz. butter
1 teaspon paprika
12 oz. button mushrooms
1 gill dry cider or light ale
salt and pepper

Season cutlets both sides and marinate in chives and cider (or ale) for 2 hours, turning at end of first hour. Drain and place in a well greased casserole, pour over them the liquid in which they marinated and cover thickly with the button mushrooms, left whole. Add butter, cover and cook at 325°F. — Regulo 3, for 1 1/2 hours. Serve immediately on a bed of green peas and surrounded by creamed potatoes sprinkled with paprika.

GRILLED CHICKEN

Lebanon

TO SERVE 4

1 *poussins,* if very small, or large ones

1 head garlic

salt

olive oil

lemon juice

Divide very small poussins down the backbone and flatten them; cut the larger poussins in half. Divide up and skin the garlic cloves and pound them with salt, and rub some of it into the pieces of chicken. Sprinkle on olive oil and lemon juice and let the chicken marinate for an hour.

If you have a charcoal grill, make it very hot — glowing. If not, use a well-heated gas or electric grill. Cook the chicken on both sides. Into the rest of the garlic pounded with salt, mix just enough oil — and a few drops of lemon juice — make a sauce as thick as thick bread sauce. Not a dish for those who do not like garlic.

(Chicken with Mayonnaise)

Lebanon

Common to most Middle East countries

TO SERVE 6

1 1/2 lb. cooked, diced chicken
12 stuffed green olives
1 pint boiling water, to which has been added rind of 1 lemon
4 oz. white grapes
1 gill double cram, whipped
2 teaspoons chopped chervil
1/2 pint special mayonnaise (see below)
2 tablespoons gelatine
2 oz. toasted slivered almonds
3 tablespoons white wine, sweet
6 oz. soft white cheese
salt and pepper

Strain water and lemon rind through butter muslin and stir in gelatine. Dissolve thoroughly. Add wine and leave aside to cool.

When partially set add chicken, mayonnaise, seasoning, almonds, olives and grapes. When partially set again pour into a wetted tube mould and chill until firm. Unmould on serving dish and surround with cos lettuce leaves crisped in ice water.

Fill centre of tube with balls made from the soft white cheese mixed with the chervil and whipped cream.

Serve with mayonnaise and croutons of toast.

To Make Mayonnaise for this Dish

1/4 pint olive oil
1/4 teaspoon salt
2 medium heaped teaspoons flour
pinch castor sugar
3 tablespoons water
1 teaspoon dry mustard
3 tablespoons tarragon vinegar
1 large egg yolk

Put dry ingredients in saucepan, add vinegar and water and stir well. Cook over gentle heat until mixture starts to bubble. Boil for 4 minutes, stirring continuously. Remove from heat, cool thoroughly, add egg yolk and whisk for 1 minute. When quite cold add oil gradually, drop by drop, until it is all used. Whisk frequently while oil is being added. Chill before serving.

STUFFED CHICKEN

Morocco

TO SERVE 6 — 8

1 chicken, about 5 lb.
1 oz. almonds, blanched and peeled
1 oz. seedless raisins
1 tablespoon honey
1 tablespoon butter
1 onion, chopped
pinch of cinnamon
pinch of saffron
pinch of ginger or *ras il hanouf*

FOR THE STUFFING

3 oz. almonds, blanched and peeled butter
4 oz. seedless raisins
pinch of ginger or *ras il hanouf*
pinch of cinnamon
pinch of saffron
salt and pepper to taste
2 tablespoons honey

To make the stuffing, fry the almonds in butter and then chop them. Mix all the ingredients for the stuffing together, adding the almonds and the butter they were fried in.

Stuff the chicken with the mixture and sew it up. Put in a saucepan with nearly enough water to cover it. Add all the remaining ingredients, bring it to the boil and cook for 40 to 50 minutes. Take out the chicken and carve it. Put the pieces in a serving dish and pour over some of the sauce. Garnish with pieces of chicken liver (you may need to get a bit more) lightly fried in butter.

ROAST CHICKEN

Lebanon

1 cup dried chick-peas
water for soaking
2 quarts water
1 cup cracked wheat
1 cup water
1 tablespoon sweet butter
1 cup blanched, toasted, chopped almonds
3 teaspoons salt
1/2 teaspoon black pepper
1 roasting chicken, about 4 pound
1/2 cup sweet butter, softened
1/2 cup hot water

SOAK peas in water to cover for 24 hours. Drain, discarding water

COMBINE peas and 2 quarts water. Simmer for 1 1/2 hours until peas are tender and water evaporated. Drain, if necessary. Reserve

SIMMER wheat in 1 cup water for 45 to 50 minutes or until tender. Add 1 tablespoon sweet butter during cooking.

CHICKEN KABAB

Lebanon and Syria

3 cups chicken, cut in 1 1/2 inch pieces
1 teaspoon vinegar
1/4 teaspoon garlic powder
1/2 cup water
4 tablespoons peanut butter
1/4 teaspoon chopped garlic
1/2 cup milk
1/2 cup chicken consomme
1 teaspoon cayenne pepper
1 teaspoon soy sauce
1 teaspoon sugar
1 bay leaf
1/4 teaspoon salt

PLACE 4 to 5 chicken pieces on skewer
MIX vinegar, garlic powder, and water
DIP chicken in vinegar and bake at 450°F for 15 minutes
COMBINE remaining ingredients in pan
COOK over low heat, stirring, until sauce thickens
SERVE hot chicken with sauce
YIELD 4 servings

CHICKEN WITH HOMMOS

Egypt

TO SERVE 4 — 6

1 chicken, about 4 lb.
salt and pepper
flour
4 oz. butter
1 large onion
3 cloves garlic
2 tablespoons tomato puree
bouquet garni
1/4 — 1/2 pint (U.S. 2/3 — 1 1/4 cups) chicken stock
8 oz. chick-peas

Cut the chicken into 8 pieces. Season, dredge in flour and cook quickly in foaming butter. Chop the onion and cook it in the butter. Chop the garlic and add it. Sauté the chicken, garlic and onion for 5 minutes. Add the tomato puree and bouquet garni, and stir. Cook for another 5 minutes. Add the chicken stock and cook briskly until the chicken is done — about 20 minutes (but test and do not overcook or it might get hard or disintegrate).

Meanwhile, or rather beforehand, you should have prepared some chick-peas by soaking them overnight and then by boiling them — skimming frequently — in salted water for about 2 hours until they are soft. Drain them and add them to the chicken. Correct the seasoning.

CHICKEN STOCK

Common to all Middle Eastern countries

1 boiling fowl, (about 2 lb.)
giblets
1 blade mace
1 teaspoon rock salt
1 onion
3 white peppercorns
1 teaspoon sweet marjoram
cold water to cover

Wash fowl inside and outside under cold running water. Put in a large saucepan, with the giblets and salt. Bring to boil and simmer for 45 minutes. Add whole onion, herbs and peppercorns and simmer for a further 3 1/2 hours. Remove fowl and giblets and strain liquor through muslin. Cool, skim fat from top and use as required within 24 hours.

The meat of the fowl can be used for any cooked chicken dishes.

SDOUR FRAREEJ (Chicken Breasts)
Lebanon
TO SERVE 6

2 lb. cooked chicken breast
4 tablespoons flour
8 oz. butter
1/2 pint single cream
1/2 teaspoon white pepper
4 oz. grated cheese
4 egg yolks
6 slices lamb's tongue
1/2 teaspoon sweet marjoram
3 tablespoons butter
6 mushrooms, halved
salt to taste

Cook mushrooms in boiling salted water for 10 minutes. Remove from heat, drain and allow to cool.

Mince chicken breast finely. Melt the 3 tablespoons butter, add flour and cook without browning for 3 minutes, stirring frequently. Add cream very slowly, stirring continuously, then add well beaten egg yolks, cheese and seasoning. Cook for 2-3 minutes until mixture is stiff. Add the chicken, mushrooms and tongue (tongue should be cut into small pieces). Combine well, remove from heat.

When cooked take small pieces, shape into sausages and fry in hot butter until golden brown on both sides. Start frying each batch at very low heat and increase gradually.

HABIBA (Chicken and Tomatoes)

Damascus

TO SERVE 4

3	large tomatoes, skinned
6	oz. chicken breast, cooked and minced
1/2	pint yoghurt dressing
6	eggs, poached
1	tablespoon parsley, minced
24	black olives, pitted

Cut the tomatoes in half and remove the pulpy insides, then put a cold poached egg in each. Arrange in a circle in a flat serving dish and heap the chicken breast in the centre. Chill for 1 hour. Mask the whole with yoghurt dressing, garnish with parsley and black olives. Serve well chilled.

RICE AND CHICKEN WITH WHITE SAUCE

Common to all Middle East countries

2 tender chickens
1 3/4 lbs. rice
5 oz. butter
3 oz. flour
4 oz. cream (light cream)
3 tsp. salt
1/4 tsp. white pepper
6 oz. grated Gruyere cheese (for the rice) a dash of nutmeg (for the sauce)
4 pts. cold water (for the chicken)
4 1/2 oz. butter (to cook the rice)

Clean chickens. Put in a pot and add 4 pts. of water with 1 tbs. salt and let boil. Remove skim and reduce heat to medium. Cook until chickens are done. Lift chicken into another container and keep covered near the heat. Strain broth and return it to pot and continue to boil it. Melt butter for the rice and cook rice, but using chicken broth instead of water and adding 1 1/2 tbs. salt, cook over moderate heat until rice is done.

To make the white sauce: Melt butter in a sauce pan. Add flour and stir with wire beater for 3 minutes. Add remainder of chicken broth and cook slowly first then boil well, add salt, pepper and nutmeg and let boil some more. Remove pot to low heat then add cream. When ready to serve, put rice in shape of round cake mould placing the chicken pieces in the centre sprinkle over it some of the sauce and the grated cheese. Serve the remaining sauce and cheese separately.

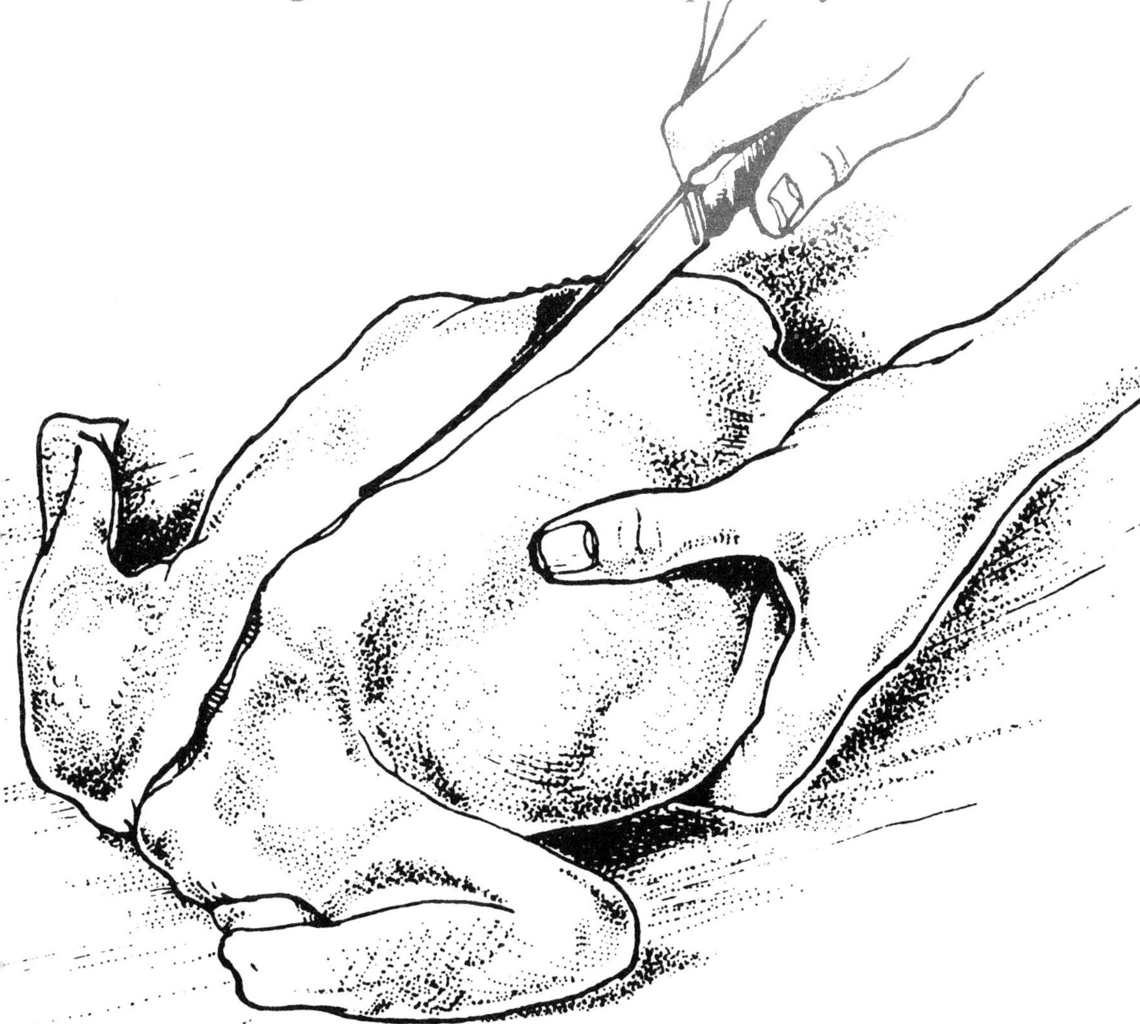

BOILED STUFFED CHICKEN

Common to all Middle East countries

TO SERVE 4

- 2 chickens and stuffing composed of the following:
- 12 oz. meat chopped
- 4 oz. rice
- 1 1/2 tbs. salt
- 1/2 tsp. spices
- 1/8 tsp. saffron
- 1 oz. cold water
- 1 tbs. rose water
- 4 oz. rice (if soup is to be made out of the chicken broth)

Prepare stuffing and prepare chicken accordingly to cook until done. Cut chicken into pieces and arrange them on top of the stuffing in a platter or shallow serving dish.

Soften the onions in a little warm oil until they are transparent and have lost their water, taking care not to let them color. Mix the meat, tomatoes, and tomato paste in a large bowl. If you are using fresh tomatoes, get rid of as much of their juice and seeds as possible, and crush them to a pulp. If you are using a can of tomatoes, drain them well, as too much liquid will make the dough soggy. Add, sugar allspice, and lemon juice, and season to taste with salt and pepper. Drain the onions of oil and add them to the meat mixture. Knead well by hand. Some people like to add chopped parsley and a little cayenne pepper as well.

The filling is sometimes varied by omitting the tomatoes altogether, and adding 1/3 cup pine nuts and 2 to 3 tablespoons tamarind.

Knead the risen dough a few times and divide it into many walnut-size balls. Allow to rest for a few minutes, then roll each piece on a lightly floured board with a lightly floured rolling pin into a round flat shape 5 to 6 inches in diameter. Alternatively, oil your hands lightly, take smaller lumps of dough, and flatten each piece as much as possible with the palm of your hand on an oiled plate.

Spread the prepared filling very generously over each piece, covering the entire surface (otherwise the filling will look meager when the pastries are baked). Transfer each round to a lightly oiled baking sheet as you prepare it.

Bake in a preheated very hot oven (450°F to 475°F) for 8 to 10 minutes only. The pastries should be well done but still white and soft enough to roll up or fold in the hand to be eaten, as some people like to do.

Lahma bi ajeen can be reheated by putting them in a warm oven for a few minutes. They can also be warmed up in the top of a double boiler. Serve with various salads.

ROAST CHICKEN WITH RICE

Bahrain

1 roasting chicken, about 4 pounds
1/2 lemon
2 teaspoons monosodium glutamate
1/2 cup softened butter
1 cup raw rice
1/2 cup minced onion
1 1/4 cups consomme
3/4 cups water
2 1/2 teaspoons salt
1 teaspoon black pepper
1/3 cup dried currants
1 teaspoon lemon juice
1 green pepper, chopped
2 tablespoons flour

RUB chicken inside and out with cut surface of lemon. Sprinkle with monosodium glutamate.
HOOK wing to back of chicken to hold neck skin. Tie legs together
RUB with 2 tablespoons softened butter
PLACE on rack in roasting pan
BAKE at 275°F for 30 minutes per pound
REMOVE chicken; keep warm
COOK rice and 1/4 cup onion in remaining butter over medium heat, stirring, until rice is browned
ADD remaining 1 teaspoon monosodium gluatamate, 3/4 cup consomme, 1 1/4 teaspoons salt, pepper, currants and lemon juice. Bring to boil. Cover
SIMMER for 12 to 15 minutes until liquid is absorbed
TURN into 4 greased 3/4 cup or 6 1/4 cup moulds.

CHICKEN—STUFFED, BOILED AND BROWNED

First, boil or brown chicken

TO SERVE 4

2 large, tender chickens
1 lb. chopped meat
5 oz. rice, soaked
2 tsp. salt
1/2 tsp. spices
5 oz. butter
2 1/2 tbs. flour
1/4 tsp. saffron

Prepare stuffing, boil or brown chicken. Just before chicken is done lift out of pot. Melt and heat butter in another pot and brown chicken on all sides. Add broth in which chicken was boiling. Cover and cook on low heat until chicken is cooked.

You can make a sauce from the broth in the following way: Take part of butter in which chicken was browned. Add flour and stir over low heat. Add broth and cook till it begins to thicken. Pour it through a fine strainer, return it to heat to come to a boil and serve in separate bowl to be used over chicken and stuffing if desired. Chicken is served by cutting it to pieces and arranging the pieces over the stuffing. A second way to serve stuffed boiled chicken is as follows:

After chicken is cooked, toast and break about 12 oz. of Arab bread in a pottery or porcelain bowl. Mash few cloves of garlic with salt and mix with some laban. Pour this mixture over the bread and mix well. Cut cooked chicken into pieces and mix it with the stuffing and make that a topping for bread mixture. If you may, use more of the laban mixed with mashed garlic and salt over the chicken and stuffing and serve.

CHICKEN WITH WALNUTS

Saudi Arabia

This recipe is highly recommended for a buffet.

1 whole chicken, about 4 pounds
2 cups water
1 onion, sliced
1 carrot, scraped and sliced
1 spring parsley
1 teaspoon salt
teaspoon black pepper
2 cups twice ground walnuts
1 tablespoon paprika
3 slices bread

PLACE chicken in water. Add onion, carrot, parsley, salt, and pepper

BRING to boil. Reduce heat

SIMMER for 40 minutes

REMOVE chicken. Cool. Discard skin and bones. Chop meat. Reserve

STRAIN chicken stock. Reserve

MIX walnuts and paprika. Press between double cheesecloth to extract oil for garnish. Reserve

1 teaspoons salt
4 tablespoons butter
1/8 teaspoon cinnamon
1/8 teaspoon cloves

1 onion, chopped
2 bay leaves
1 1/2 cups water
parsley

SPRINKLE chicken with 1 teaspoon salt
BROWN in melted butter in skillet on all sides
ADD 1 1/2 teaspoons salt and remaining ingredients, except parsley. Bring to a boil
REDUCE heat. Cover. Simmer for 40 minutes.

BUKHARI CHICKEN

Mecca

1 chicken, 2 1/2 — 3 1/2 pounds, cut in serving pieces
1 teaspoon monosodium glutamate
1 teaspoon salt
1 1/2 cups bouillon
1/4 cup butter
1 tablespoon soy sauce
1/2 teaspoon ground ginger
1 cup diced celery
1 onion, sliced
1 green pepper, cut in thin strips
1 can (4 ounces) sliced mushrooms
2 tablespoons cornstarch
cup water
1 cup shredded cabbage

SPRINKLE chicken with monosodium glutamate and salt

BROWN in melted butter in skillet on all sides

ADD bouillon, soy sauce, ginger, and celery. Cover

SIMMER for 25 minutes

ADD onion, green pepper, and mushrooms with liquid. Cover

SIMMER for 10 minutes

ADD blended cornstarch and water. Cook, stirring, until thickened
ADD cabbage. Cover
COOK for 3 minutes
YIELD 4 servings

CHICKEN MOHALLABIYYA
Saudi Arabia
TO SERVE 4
1 chicken
12 cups (2,400cc water)
1 1/2 cups rice (do not use Uncle Ben's)
1 teaspoon salt
One big onion
dash of pepper to your desire
dash of cinnamon to your desire
Wash and clean chicken. Put the chicken and the onion in pot. Cover with water and bring to boil. Reduce heat.
Simmer for 2-3 hours until tender. Reserve soup. Remove bones from chicken. Cut into pieces and sprinkle with salt.

Wash rice. Add 10 cups of soup from above. Cook over low heat for 1 hour, or until tender. Add chicken meat to pot. Then add salt, pepper and cinnamon as desired.

ROAST CHICKEN WITH PINE-NUT STUFFING

Lebanon and Syria

1/2 cup pine nuts
1 chicken liver, chopped
3 tablespoons butter
1/2 cup dried currants
2 teaspoons salt, divided
2 1/4 cups boiling water
1 cup raw rice
1 roasting chicken, about 4 pounds
1/4 cup butter, softened

SAUTÉ nuts and liver in 1 tablespoon butter until nuts turn pink

ADD 1 teaspoon currants, 1 teaspoon salt, boiling water, and rice. Cover

SIMMER for 25 minutes or until water is absorbed

ADD 2 tablespoons butter. Mix well.

WASH and dry chicken. Sprinkle cavity with remaining salt. Rub outside with softened butter

STUFF chicken with rice mixture

PLACE on rack in shallow roasting pan

ROAST at 375°F

YIELD 4 to 6 servings

SUGGESTED MENU: Roast Chicken with

Pine-Nut Stuffing, braised celery, cucumber salad, chocolate cake, coffee.

(Stuffed Turkey)

Lebanon

TO SERVE 6—8

1 young turkey, 6 lbs.
3 onions, chopped finely
2 cloves crushed garlic
8 oz. Patna rice
2 carrots, quartered
1 tablespoon pine kernels
1/2 teaspoon basil
salt to taste
a little good stock
1/2 pint lemon water (juice of 1 lemon added to just under 1/2 pint water)
6 springs dill
1 tablespoon dried blackcurrants
9 tablespoons butter
2 tomatoes, skinned and chopped
1/2 teaspoon white pepper
1 tablespoon red wine

Put cleaned turkey into a large saucepan with lemon water, 5 tablespoons butter, 2 onions, carrots, garlic. Cover and bring to boil. Remove from heat immediately and keep hot.

Put bird in large meat tray, with liquor and vegetables from saucepan and cook until bird is tender in a medium oven, (350°F. — Regulo 3). Baste from time to time with own juices. When bird is nicely and evenly browned remove from oven and keep hot.

Strain fat and vegetable juices into a saucepan. Increase amount to 3/4 pint liquid by adding the wine and a little good stock. Leave this liquor aside for it will be used for the rice stuffing.

Meanwhile, cut up liver and heart of bird into small pieces, sauté in a little of remaining butter for 3 minutes. Keep hot by side of fire.

Clean rice with almost boiling water, leave to get cold, then wash under running water and drain.

Melt 2 tablespoons of butter, add 1 more onion, finely chopped, and pine kernels and fry for 5 minutes until both are pale brown. Add rice and cook a further 8 to 10 minutes over medium heat. Add the 3/4 pint liquor, blackcurrants, tomatoes, herbs and seasoning, cover and cook over reduced heat until all liquid has been absorbed by rice, about 12 to 15 minutes. Add minced dill, liver and heart, combine well and remove from heat. Stuff turkey tightly with mixture, put in warm oven for 40 minutes and serve.

SAMAK MAKLY (Fried Fish)

Syria

TO SERVE 6

1 1/2 lb. any white fish

1 large egg

1 lemon juice

1 onion, sliced

1 teaspoon coriander seed

4 oz. plain flour (seasoned with pinch bay leaf)

1 teaspoon cayenne pepper

6 peppercorns

1 sliced carrot

1 clove crushed garlic
3 pints water
1 large onion
1/2 pint olive oil
2 thick slices white bread, crusts removed
salt
little milk for moistening

Put cleaned fish, onion, carrot and peppercorns in water and cook for 15 minutes at simmering point. Raise heat and boil for 2 or 3 minutes more. Remove fish from liquid, flake off from bones and put in a mixing bowl.

Soak bread in milk for a few minutes then squeeze dry with hands. Mix with the flaked fish. Add unbeaten egg, onion, juice, coriander seed, garlic, salt and cayenne pepper. Knead together. Take small pieces of mixture and roll in the hands to finger shape. Coat with seasoned flour and fry in sizzling hot olive oil until golden brown. Serve hot or cold with fresh lemon juice, new potatoes and diced beetroot.

(Red Mullet in the Oven)

Common to most Middle East countries

TO SERVE 6

6 red mullet
6 springs chopped parsley
salt and pepper
greaseproof paper
2 tablespoons corn oil
1 lemon juice
few tablespoons melted butter

Clean, wash and pat fish dry, leaving on heads and tails. Make a slit in one side and clean out insides. Wash well under running water.

Take double greaseproof paper, brush thoroughly with melted butter. Wrap fish in this, secure with string, put on baking sheet and cook in a hot oven (400°F. — Regulo 6) for 45 minutes.

Mix parsley, lemon juice, corn oil and seasoning and sprinkle over each fish just before serving.

FISH KEBAB

Egypt

TO SERVE 4

1 1/2 lb. fillets of sea bream
3 onions
3 lemons
4 bay leaves
salt and pepper
1/2 teaspoon cumin
1 lb. tomatoes

Cut up the fish into pieces about the same size as you would for a lamb kebab and put them into a bowl. Chop the onions and squeeze out their juice through a muslin cloth on to the pieces of fish. Squeeze in the juice of lemons. Put in the bay leaves, salt, pepper and cumin and let the pieces of fish marinate for an hour or so in a cool place. Cut the tomatoes into quarters.

On skewers put pieces of marinated fish, bay leaves and tomatoes. Brush them with olive oil and grill them on hot charcoal. Serve them on a bed of parsley with quarters of lemon.

STEAMED FISH

Saudi Arabia

TO SERVE 4

Ingredients:

1 black sea bream
1/2 stalk green onion
1 slice ginger
1 lemon juice
2 tablespoons soup stock
1/2 tablespoon sugar
1 teaspoon salt
2 tablespoons vinegar
1 tablespoon tomato ketchup

cooking time 30 minutes

Sauce:

dash of ginger powder

Clean fish. Score both sides. Place cut green onion and ginger inside.

Slice lemon and arrange it around the fish. Pour sauce over fish.

Steam for 30 minutes.

MACARONI WITH WHITE FISH

Arabian Gulf countries

TO SERVE 6

8 oz. macaroni
8 oz. any cooked white fish
2 green peppers, chopped
1/4 pint olive oil
salt to taste
3 quarts boiling salted water
2 shallots, minced
1 clove crushed garlic
1 teaspoon cayenne pepper
1 pint tomato juice

Break macaroni in 2-inch pieces and cook for 10 minutes in fast boiling water. Drain, rinse in hot water and drain again thoroughly.

Heat oil and cook the shallots, peppers, garlic and macaroni for 15 minutes over moderate heat, stirring from time to time to prevent burning. Remove from heat.

Heat the tomato juice, season and stir in the flaked fish. Stir this mixture into the macaroni mixture. Put the whole thing into an oiled baking dish, cover and bake at 350°F. — Regulo 3, for 35 minutes. Serve immediately.

SAYYADIYYA

Common to all Middle East countries

TO SERVE 4

5 lbs. 7 1/2 oz. fish (bass)
7 oz. onions cut in shape of wings
10 oz. oil (olive oil perferred)
1 lb. 5 oz. rice, cleaned and soaked in warm water
2 pts. 12 oz. boiling water
2 1/2 tsp. salt
1/2 tsp. cumin

Salt water in a bowl at the rate of 3 1/2 tbs. salt to 2 pts. of water. Clean the fish and put it for an hour in the salt water. Put oil in a large skillet and let it become hot; add onions and fry them till they become very dark (but not burnt) turning them constantly. Add onions to the boiling water and allow to cook until very soft. Pour into a strainer; mash onions through the strainer into the water. This should be placed in a pot large enough to hold the fish which is now added with the salt. Allow to boil about 40 minutes.

Remove fish from broth and add the rice; it boils briskly first then reduce to moderate heat till rice is cooked. Serve the rice on a platter and the fish on another dish. A little cumin may be

added to the rice if desired.

Note: After removing fish from broth, about 4/5 pt. of broth may be taken out to which add the juice of two lemons and boil a little. This becomes the sauce to be served over the rice and fish.

FISH SALAD

Lebanon

TO SERVE 4

1 lb. white fish
3 tablespoons olive oil
pinch crushed bay leaf
6 sliced green olives
1 oz. stoned raisins
8 oz. Patna rice
1 chopped onion
1 chopped dessert apple
4 finely chopped anchovies
2 sliced tomatoes

Steam the fish until tender, drain and leave aside to cool. Flake flesh from bone.

Boil rice in just enough water to cover. When soft and fluffy drain and wash several times in cold water.

Cook onion and bayleaf in the olive oil until transparent but not brown. Stir into rice. Add the fish, anchovies, apples and raisins. Arrange on a long dish, decorate with sliced olives and tomatoes, and serve very cold sprinkled with lemon juice.

TROUT WITH CREAM

Kuwait

TO SERVE 6

6 trout
1 gill sour cream
salt and freshly ground pepper
3 tablespoons butter
1/4 pint double cream
1 teaspoon sweet marjoram

Clean fish and pat dry. Lay in buttered fireproof dish, add butter and marjoram. Bake at 350°F. — Regulo 3, for about 25 minutes.

Stir the double cream into the sour cream and pour over the fish. Bake for a further 10 minutes at same temperature. Serve at once.

SAMACH HAR (Chilled Salmon)

Kuwait

TO SERVE 6

3 lb. middle-cut salmon
few springs parsley
olive oil for frying
lemon juice

Wash and dry salmon and cut into 6 pieces.

Heat oil in deep pan and cook salmon until golden brown and cooked right through, about 12 minutes for each slice. Drain on greaseproof paper and allow to cool.

Serve cold, brushed with lemon juice, and garnished with the parsley.

MACKEREL IN OLIVE OIL

Common to all Middle East countries

TO SERVE 6

4 medium size mackerel
5 sliced onions
1/2 gill dry white wine
1 teaspoon paprika
3/4 pint court-bouillon
5 cloves halved garlic
1 tablespoon tomato puree
1 pint olive oil
1 sliced carrot
salt to taste

Scale and clean insides of fish but leave on heads and tails.

Heat half the oil in a wide bottomed pan, add onions and cook over medium heat for 15 minutes. Add carrot and garlic and cook another 15 minutes. Remove pan from heat, add rest of oil, paprika, tomato puree (thinned with water), wine, court-bouillon and seasoning. Cover and cook for further 20 minutes over moderate heat. Uncover and boil rapidly for 7 minutes to reduce liquor. Remove from heat and strain through muslin.

Arrange mackerel side by side in liquor, cover with a napkin — which must not touch fish — and put on lid. Cook on low heat for 25 to 30 minutes, remove from heat and allow to cool in pan. Serve very cold but not iced.

FISH RICE

Lebanon

Ingredients:

8 oz. oil
17 oz. boiling water
1 1/10 lbs. onions cut wing shape, which has been fried in oil until a golden colour
5 oz. snobar (pine nuts)
2 tbs. salt
1/2 tsp. saffron
1 lb. 7 oz. rice

Heat oil in skillet and brown snobar. Remove snobar from oil and put onions in oil to fry until a golden colour. Lift a large portion of the fried onions. Transfer the oil and remaining onions from the skillet into a cooking pot, add rice, salt and saffron and stir well over high heat. Add boiling water and let it boil hard first, then reduce heat and cook slowly until rice is done. Serve on a platter and garnish with the fried snobar and onions.

FISH WITH RICE

Saudi Arabia

1 3-lb. fish
3 cups uncooked rice
1 cup olive oil
4 tbs. butter
2 onions, sliced
1 spring parsley
1 carrot
1 tbs. pine seeds
1/4 tsp. cinnamon
1/2 tsp. pepper
1 1/2 tsp. salt
1 tbs. blanched almonds
1 tsp. lemon juice
blended flour

Wash the fish and cut it into 3 to 4 pieces. Salt them thoroughly. Heat the oil well and sauté lightly the blanched almonds and pine seeds. Remove them to a separate plate. In the same pan brown the pieces of fish and set them aside. Place the sauteed fish in a heavy cooking pot, add parsley and carrot and cover them with water. Bring it to a boil, reduce the heat and simmer for 15 minutes or until the fish is tender. Remove them to a separate place. Use the same oil for frying the sliced onions until they are golden coloured. Mash the onions into the fish broth and strain it, removing the solids. Reserve aside around 2 1/2 cups of fish broth to use for cooking the rice.

2 cups uncooked rice
2 tbs. butter
3 cups water
2 tsp. salt

Wash and soak the rice in hot water for 1 hour. Melt the butter in a cooking pot and add the water and salt. Cover and bring to a boil. Drain the rice and add it to the hot water. Cover and cook on high heat for 5 minutes or until the rice begins to absorb the water. Reduce the heat and simmer without further stirring until the water is absorbed completely and perforations appear. Stir gently when ready to serve. Allow the rice to settle on the side of the stove for 5 minutes before serving.

CURRIED SHRIMP WITH TOMATO SAUCE

Bahrain

2 medium onions, chopped
1 garlic clove, minced
2 tablespoons butter
2 tablespoons curry powder
1/2 teaspoon salt
1 can (8 ounces) tomato sauce
1 cup chicken stock
3 tablespoons lemon juice
1/2 cup light cream
2 pounds shrimp, cooked, shelled and deveined
3 cups hot cooked rice
2 cups hot cooked peas
chutney and toasted almonds (for garnish)

COOK onions and garlic in butter in saucepan until tender
BLEND in curry power and salt
ADD tomato sauce and chicken stock. Cover. Simmer for 20 minutes.
STIR in lemon juice, then cream
ADD shrimp. Reheat
SERVE with rice mixed with peas
GARNISH with chutney and toasted almonds
YIELD 4 to 5 servings

SHRIMP WITH RICE

Bahrain

4 slices bacon, cut into 1-inch pieces
1 cup raw rice
1 cup sliced onions
1 garlic clove, minced
1 can (1 pound) tomatoes
1 cup water
1 teaspoon salt
teaspoon black pepper
1 1/2 pounds raw shrimp shelled and deveined

COOK bacon in skillet until crisp. Drain on absorbent paper, crumble, and reserve
ADD rice, onions, and garlic to bacon drippings
COOK over low heat, stirring, until rice is browned
ADD tomatoes, water, salt, and pepper. Mix
ADD shrimp
COVER. Simmer for 25 to 30 minutes
SPRINKLE with bacon
YIELD 4 servings

SHRIMP FRIED RICE

Kuwait

This is a good way of using leftover rice.

2 cups cooked rice
3 tablespoon bacon drippings
2 eggs, beaten
2 cups chopped, cooked shrimp
1/2 teaspoon salt
1/8 teaspoon black pepper
1 tablespoon soy sauce
1/2 teaspoon monosodium glutamate
whole cooked shrimp (garnish)
chopped parsley
pineapple slices

SAUTÉ rice in drippings in skillet for 2 minutes
ADD eggs. Stir rapidly until mixed
ADD next 5 ingredients. Heat
MOLD by pressing into bowl and turning out on serving dish
GARNISH with additional whole cooked shrimp and
GARNISH with tomato slices and parsley
YIELD 3 servings

SHRIMP AND RICE

Eastern Province — *Saudi Arabia*

1/2 cup diagonally sliced celery
1/2 cup julienne green beans
4 scallions, thinly sliced
3 tablespoons oil
1 tablespoon soy sauce
2 cups small cooked shrimp
2 eggs, beaten
hot cooked rice

SAUTÉ celery, beans, and half the scallions in oil for 3 minutes, stirring frequently
STIR in soy sauce
ADD shrimp and eggs. Stir over low heat until egg is cooked
SPRINKLE with remaining scallions
SERVE over hot cooked rice
YIELD 4 servings
SUGGESTED MENU: Sectioned grapefruit, chicken consomme, Shrimp and Rice, almond cakes, tea.

ATAIF/ARAB PANCAKES

Ataif *is a sweet dearly loved all over the Arab world, a medieval dish which has remained unchanged to this day.*

Ataif are basically pancakes dipped in syrup. Sometimes they are sprinkled with pistachios and eaten with thick cream, sometimes piled high on a platter in a pyramid of alternate layers of ataif and cream. Or they may also be stuffed with chopped walnuts, sugar and cinnamen.

They are eaten as often as possible although it is the special sweet of the Id es-Saghir after the fast of Ramadan. It is also a wedding sweet.

Families nowadays usually buy their ataif ready-made from bakeries, and then stuff them and dip them in syrup. But the batter is easy enough to make at home. Several people make it themselves. None have weights, not do they measure quantities. They just look at the batter and add more water or more flour if they think it requires it.

The recipe below will make about 36 ataif.

BATTER

1/2 oz. (1 cake) fresh yeast or
1/2 oz. (1 package) dried yeast
1 teaspoon sugar

1 1/4 cups lukewarm water
1 1/2 cups all-purpose flour
SYRUP
2 1/2 cups sugar
1 1/4 cups water
1 tablespoon lemon juice
1-2 tablespoons orange blossom water
Oil
Whipped cream or clotted cream
Chopped pistachio nuts or almonds

Dissolve the yeast with 1 teaspoon sugar in 1/4 cup lukewarm water. Allow it to stand in a warm place for 10 minutes, or until it begins to bubble. Sift the flour into a large bowl. Add the yeast mixture and work it into the flour. Add the remaining water gradually, stiring constantly, until the batter is smooth. Leave the bowl in a warm place, covered with a cloth, for about 1 hour. The soft, almost liquid batter will rise and become bubbly and a little elastic.

ATAIF WITH CHEESE

Ataif (pancakes) are extremely popular served sweet, stuffed with nuts and doused with syrup. A more uncommon but most excellent way of preparing them is to stuff them with cheese.

Prepare ataif, following the recipe, and adding a little salt to the batter instead of sugar. Greek Halumi cheese is my favorite filling for savory *ataif.*

Fill with a small slice of Halumi cheese or mozzarella; or make a filling with 1/2 lb. grated Cruyere, Wensleydala, Gouda, Edam, or Canadian Cheddar, 1 whole egg and black pepper to taste. Mix the ingredients thoroughly with a fork.

Put a heaped teaspoon of filling in the centre of each little ataif on the soft, unfried side. Fold the pancake over the filling to make a half-moon shape and seal the edges by pinching them together with your fingers. The soft, moist dough will stick together.

Deep-fry in hot oil until golden and drain on absorbent paper. Serve hot or cold, preferably hot.

An alternative cheese filling is made with feta, with white Greek cheese, crumbled with a fork, seasoned with white pepper, and mixed with a

few finely chopped chives. Ordinary white cream cheeses will not do, since they invariably melt and ooze out.

The ataif can be eaten flat, as they are. Dip each one in the cold syrup and spread with thick cream. In the Middle East a cream made from buffalo's milk called *eishta* is used. You may, instead, use whipped cream or clotted cream. Sprinkle chopped pistachios or almonds over the cream. Serve 3 or 4 person.

A beautiful way of serving ataif at a party is to make the plain ataif, fry them on both sides, and dip them in syrup as above. Put a layer of ataif on a round serving dish, spread it with *eishta* (no other cream will do), and sprinkle with chopped pistachios or almonds. Repeat several times, making a pyramid, and ending with a layer of cream and nuts.

STUFFED ATAIF

The stuffed ataif are the most exquisite ones. When making these, remember to fry one side of the pancakes only (the other side must remain moist so that its edges can be stuck together). Pile them up on a plate as you make them.

1. ATAIF STUFFED WITH CHEESE

Put a tablespoon of cheese on the unfried side of each pancake. Clotted cream and whipped cream are not suitable in this case, as they would melt and ooze out when fried. (An unsalted cheese such as Italian ricotta may, however, be used). Fold it in half and pinch the edges together firmly to seal them, making a half-moon shape and trapping the filling.

Drop each pancake in very hot oil and deep-fry for 2 to 3 minutes until a pale golden color. Remove with a perforated spoon. Drain well on absorbent paper. Dip the hot pancakes in syrup and serve hot or cold. If you have a very sweet tooth, serve them with the syrup poured over them.

2. ATAIF STUFFED WITH NUTS

Make a filling of 1/2 lb. (2 cups) shelled walnuts, chopped, 4 tablespoons sugar, and 2 teaspoons ground cinnamon. Stuff and deep-fry the pancakes as above.

Make a syrup by dissolving the sugar in water with lemon juice and simmering it until it is thick enough to coat the back of a spoon. Stir in orange blossom water and simmer for 2 minutes longer. Allow it to cool, then chill in the refrigerator.

When the batter is ready, dip a piece of cotton or paper towel in oil and rub a heavy frying pan with it so as to grease it with a very thin film of oil. Heat the pan until it is very hot, then reduce the heat and keep it at medium.

Pour 1 tablespoon of batter into the pan, tilting the pan a little to allow it to spread. It will not spread out too much and will remain in a small, round, fattish shape. (Do not try to spread it out too much). When the pancake loses its whiteness, becomes bubbly, and comes away from the pan easily, lift it out with a palette knife. Fry one side of the pancake only if you are making stuffed pancakes. Otherwise, flip it over and cook the other side.

Put the pancakes aside in a pile on a plate. They should be somewhat thick and spongy.

BAYRAM PASTA (Festival Cake)

Syria

6 squares plain chocolate
2 oz. self-raising flour
2 oz. soft butter
little over 3 tablespoons brandy
2 oz. vanilla sugar (keep vanilla pod in sugar jar)
4 egg whites
4 egg yolks
pinch salt

Melt chocolate in very little hot water, stir until smooth and creamy.

Cream butter and sugar. Beat egg yolks with salt until thick and lemon coloured, then stir into creamed butter mixture. Add melted chocolate very slowly.

Sift flour 3 times and stir into mixture alternately with brandy. Fold in last of all the stiffly beaten egg whites. Pour into an oiled 9-inch square tin and bake at 345°F. — Regulo 3, for about 50 minutes. Test with knife to make sure it is cooked.

Cool on a wire rack, split in halves and decorate top and inside with Chikolata.

BANANA LOAF

Palestine

3 oz. butter
8 oz. self-raising flour
3 egg yolks
few drops banana essence
3 oz. soft brown sugar
1 gill milk
3 egg whites
3 large bananas

Cream the butter and sugar, beat egg yolks for 5 minutes and add to the butter mixture. Add milk and then the flour. Stir well and add the bananas, mashed, and banana essence. Beat egg whites stiffly and fold in.

Bake at 350°F. — Regulo 3, for 1 hour and serve cold, sliced and spread with a little butter.

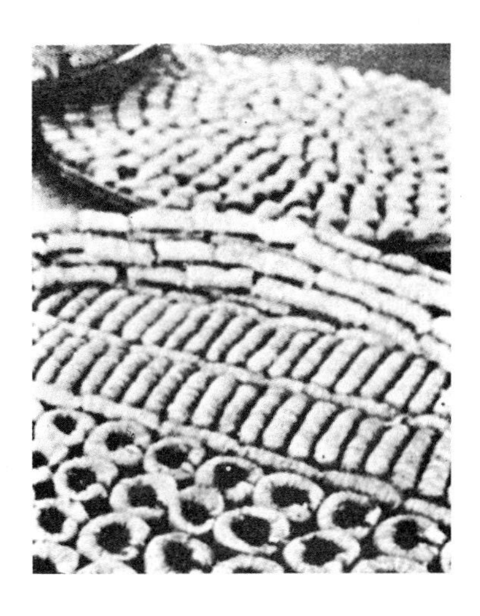

ARABIAN NIGHTS ICING

Egypt

3 tablespoons soft butter, unsalted
12 oz. sifted icing sugar
1 large egg yolk
1 1/2 tablespoons very strong hot coffee
1 tablespoon single cream
1/2 tablespoon cocoa

Cream the butter and add egg yolk, beat for 2 minutes with a fork. Add sugar and cocoa very gradually (the cocoa should have been sifted with the sugar) and mix in the hot coffee. Add the cream and beat with a fork to a smooth spreading consistency.

ARABIAN NIGHTS GATEAU

Egypt

2 oz. soft butter, unsalted
3 eggs
1/2 teaspoon baking powder
1/2 teaspoon cinnamon
1 gill yoghurt
2 oz. ground sweet almonds
3 oz. vanilla sugar
4 oz. self-raising flour
1/2 teaspoon nutmeg
1 tablespoon cocoa
1 teaspoon lemon juice

Cream butter and sugar until white and fluffy. Beat the eggs for 2 minutes, then beat into the butter and sugar. Sift the dry ingredients 3 times, excepting the almonds, and stir in alternately with the whisked yoghurt and lemon juice. Stir in ground almonds last of all. Pour mixture into 2 greased 8-inch tins and bake at 350°F. Regulo 3, for 40 minutes.

Cool and fill with Arabian Nights icing.

BANANA CAKE

Lebanon

2 oz. castor sugar
2 eggs
4 bananas
1/2 teaspoon baking soda
2 oz. almonds, finely chopped
4 oz. soft butter
3 tablespoons sour cream
8 oz. self-raising flour
pinch salt
1/2 tablespoon rosewater

Cream butter and sugar until light and fluffy. Beat eggs and salt together for 2 minutes then beat into butter mixture. Stir in the whisked sour cream, rosewater and pulped bananas.

Sift flour and soda and stir in carefully with the almonds.

Pour mixture into an oiled cake tin, leave to rest for 30 minutes, then bake at 350°F. — Regulo 3, for about 40 minutes. Test first with a knife and if it comes out clean the cake is cooked.

Cool on a wire rack and sprinkle top with icing sugar.

RICE CAKE

Common to all Middle East countries

4 oz. plain flour
4 oz. ground rice
2 oz. sultanas
1 oz. currants
2 eggs
1 teaspoon baking powder
1 gill milk
3 oz. butter
3 oz. soft brown sugar
2 oz. seedless raisins, halved
1 tablespoon lemon rind
pinch salt

Sift flour, salt and baking soda and rub in the butter. Add all the fruit, ground rice and lemon rind and mix well.

Rotary beat eggs for 3 minutes and add to milk and stir into the dry ingredients. Mix well and put into a greased 7-inch tin. Bake at 350°F. — Regulo 3, for about 1 1/2 hours, although a test should be made after 1 1/4 hours.

APRICOT CAKE

Damascus

1 lb. self-raising flour
5 oz. butter
5 eggs
1 teaspoon nutmeg
1 gill milk
6 oz. castor sugar
8 oz. apricot jam
1 tablespoon cinnamon
pinch ground cloves

Cream the butter and sugar and add the well beaten eggs. Add jam and beat into mixture until smooth. Sift flour and spices and add alternately with the milk.

Bake at 350°F. — Regulo 3, for about 1 1/2 hours or until a knife test shows that the cake is cooked.

TORTELLA (Chocolate Torte)

Syria

5 oz. butter
5 oz. flour
chocolate filling
5 oz. sugar
5 egg yolks
5 oz. grated chocolate
5 egg whites

Cream butter and sugar until light and fluffy, add flour and egg yolks alternately. Rotary beat for 7 minutes. Add the grated chocolate, stir and fold in the stiffly beaten egg whites.

Bake at 350°F. — Regulo 3, for 35 minutes, until nicely browned and firm to the touch. Cool on a rack, cut into 2 and spread with chocolate filling.

CHILEK (Strawberry Icing)

Common to most Middle East countries

1 lb. ripe strawberries
3 oz. unsalted butter
1 1/2 lb. sifted icing sugar
1/2 teaspoon lemon juice

Pulp the strawberries and then put through a fine sieve. Put in a bowl and add the lemon juice.

Cream butter and add icing sugar by degrees, then combine with the pulped strawberries. Use as icing for small cakes.

COOKING COURSE IN BEIRUT

KARAMELA (A Caramel Cream Sweet with Apricots)
Lebanon
TO SERVE 6

4 oz. rice
1/2 pint single cream
3 oz. soft brown sugar
1 teaspoon nutmeg
1 pint milk
2 oz. butter
1 lb. cooked apricots, stoned

Wash and clean rice and simmer in the milk for 20 minutes. Add cream and simmer another 15 minutes. Add butter and sugar and stir until sugar is dissolved. Remove from heat.

Spread a layer of rice on bottom of a greased pie dish, then add a layer of apricots. Repeat the process until dish is full, finishing off with a layer of rice. Bake at 350°F. — Regulo 3, until nicely browned. Sprinkle with nutmeg and serve cold.

HYTALIYYAH WITH BANANAS

Syria, Lebanon, Palestine

TO SERVE 4

2 tablespoons butter
3 eggs
1/2 pint juice from white grapes
1/2 tablespoon arrowroot
8 oz. castor sugar
1 tablespoon ground rice
1/2 pint olive oil
4 oz. flour, well sifted
pinch salt
3 bananas, cut lengthwise

Boil sugar and grape juice for 15 minutes, uncovered, and stirring all the time until sugar is dissolved. Remove from heat and leave aside.

Melt butter and add wine and salt. Bring to boil gradually. Add the flour, a little at a time, and cook on low heat for 8 minutes, stirring continuously. Remove from heat and add ground rice and arrowroot (both previously mixed to a thin paste with little water). Mix thoroughly and leave to cool.

When almost cold add the eggs and knead for about 8 minutes, then put into a forcing bag with a 1/3-inch nozzle.

Heat olive oil a little and pipe 2 inch lengths of the mixture into it. Cook on low heat until they begin to swell, then increase heat to moderate and cook until both sides are golden brown. If more than one batch has to be cooked, remember to cool off olive oil before starting another batch and never increase the heat until swelling has begun.

Toss the cooked sweetmeats in the syrup, leave for 5 minutes, remove and drain and serve cold with the sliced bananas.

QAHWAT EL HADAR (Coffee Cream Icing or Filling)

Common to all Middle East countries

4 oz. unsalted butter
1 tablespoon single cream
1 tablespoon pistachio nuts, finely chopped
8 tablespoons castor sugar
few drops good coffee essence
1 tablespoon hot water

Cream the butter and sugar until smooth and creamy, beat in the cream and the pistachio nuts. Add hot water and beat again, then stir in the essence.

MANDALINA (An Orange Sweet)

Egypt

TO SERVE 6

- 3 eggs
- 1/2 pint sour cream
- 1 teaspoon baking powder
- 1 1/2 pints water
- 12 oz. soft brown sugar
- 1/4 pint whipped cream
- 6 oz. castor sugar
- 4 oz. self-raising flour, sifted
- 1 tablespoon grated orange rind
- 1 tablespoon orange juice

few slices orange for decoration.

Mix together the water, brown sugar and orange juice, put in a saucepan and bring to boil rather slowly, stirring until sugar has dissolved. Increase heat and boil rapidly, uncovered, for 15 minutes. Leave aside.

With a rotary beater beat eggs and sugar together until sugar has dissolved. Add sour cream, the flour sifted with the baking powder, and orange rind and beat for 5 minutes. Pour mixture into a greased baking dish and bake for 35 minutes at 400°F. — Regulo 5. Remove from oven and cut into squares in the pan. Pour the hot syrup over, cover pan and leave aside until all syrup has been absorbed.

Arrange squares on serving dish and chill thoroughly. Serve decorated with orange and a few slices and a few blobs of whipped cream.

BAKED GURNET

Egypt

TO SERVE 6

2 medium size gurnet
2 oranges
salt and pepper
1 lemon juice
2 tablespoons corn oil

Cut off gills and fins of fish, empty out and wash well. Leave heads on but remove the eyes.

Lay fish in a well greased fireproof dish, season well, add lemon juice with corn and arrange slices of orange over top. Cover with greased paper and cook for 35 minutes at 400°F. — Regulo 6. Serve on a bed of rice.

CHIKOLATA (Chocolate Icing)

Syria and Lebanon

6 oz. sifted icing sugar
2 oz. soft butter
4 tablespoons melted plain chocolate
sufficient brandy to bring to spreading consistency

Combine all ingredients and stir to a smooth texture. Use for filling or icing of cakes.

INDEX